Imprint

© Jan Sammeck, Frankfurt am Main 2023

All rights reserved

Contact the author for feedback and inquiries: hotelmarketing@sammeck.me

ISBN: 9781798527870

Online Marketing for Hotels: The Definitive Guide to Direct Distribution

How to get the most out of your advertising money and boost website revenue

Contents

1. Introduction 5
   - 1.1. Who Should Read This Book? 5
   - 1.2. Why Online Marketing for Hotels? 9
   - 1.3. Basic Definitions and Starting Points 13
2. Online Marketing - The Hotelier's Choice 20
   - 2.1. Effective but Expensive: Metasearch 20
   - 2.2. A Marketer's Favorite: Search Engine Marketing 33
   - 2.3. The Trump Card: Search Engine Optimization 41
   - 2.4. Mining for Gold: Social Media Marketing 49
   - 2.5. A Dream of Efficiency: Email-Marketing 62
   - 2.6. Good Bang for the Buck: Affiliate Marketing 73
   - 2.7. A Sledgehammer for Cracking Nuts: Display Marketing 82
   - 2.8. Creative Works: Content Marketing 91
   - 2.9. The Quick Win: Local Information Services 98
3. All Tinsel and Glitter - A Critical View on Current Hypes 100

- 3.1. Influencer Marketing 100
- 3.2. Programmatic Advertising 108
- 3.3. Fixed Fee Affiliate Marketing: The Media Partner Model 112
- 3.4. Big Data and Data Driven Marketing.................115
- 4. Managing for Success - How to Get the Most out of Ad Spend 120
  - 4.1. Limitations of Marketing Budget Allocation..121
  - 4.2. Cost-of-Sale Management 127
  - 4.3. Cost Differentials and Channel Dependencies in Online Marketing..139
  - 4.4. Without Rate Parity, Everything is Nothing...149
  - 4.5. Timing of Marketing Measures............................157
  - 4.6. Online Marketing for Mobile................................164
  - 4.7. Vouchers & Promotional Codes...........................168
  - 4.8. A Hotel Website is a Shop, not a Digital Brochure 171
  - 4.9. A Brief Excursion Into A/B-Testing...................175
- 5. Closing Words..181

1. Introduction

1.1. Who Should Read This Book?

This book intends to reach a very specific audience: hoteliers and online marketers working in the hospitality industry. Within this audience, it aims at reaching those individuals with the dedication and drive to take their online distribution to the next level. If you are interested in gaining a deeper understanding of the means available to hotels in online marketing, and learning about proven concepts to improve the management of your digital marketing, then this book is for you. It is not so much a theoretical treatise as it is a practical guidebook, seeking to give its reader stimulus and motivation to apply the concepts presented. It follows that it does not explain online marketing from scratch, at least some familiarity with e-commerce and online marketing is necessary to fully understand the underlying framework of this book.

Although there is a large number of books on online marketing available, few address the abundant specifics of the hotel industry, and none do so from a perspective that is comprehensive in the strategic sense. However, in order to take advantage of direct booking opportunities, a strategic and industry specific view on the mechanisms and interlinkages of all forms of online marketing is necessary. It is the goal of this book to provide its reader with such an understanding, by drawing on professional experience and illustrating the logical and technical context of online marketing for hotels. It aims at providing a comprehensible view on the subject matter, lined with the general and globally applicable laws of online marketing, without digressing into theoretical subtleness.

It is common in contemporary literature on management and marketing to promise easy solutions that anyone can implement in short time and see immediate success. Most often, such guides come in the form of lists like "10 easy steps for generating massive returns from your advertising money" or "15 insider scoops on how to beat competition online" etc. By trend, these books do not go beyond stating obvious trivialities or explaining the really super-basic links on a given subject.

This book is not of this kind. It is my firm conviction that serious management literature can (and should!) only promise to broaden the reader's understanding of the subject at hand, in providing him with deeper insights gained by reflecting theory on practical experience. This iterative process of calibration is what - in my view - strategy development is about: to take theoretical concepts, apply them in practice to see what really works, and then using the insights gained in adjusting one's overall business strategy. This book will present proven-to-work concepts, however, their application requires reflection on the individual circumstances to find out what combination of concepts is most useful for generating direct bookings. Thus, if you are seeking to gain a deeper understanding of the mechanisms that drive direct bookings and want to derive a sustainable long-term strategy, then this book is for you.

The intention is to provide decision makers in the hotel industry with a framework for setting up distribution via their own brand.com website in order to build up independence from online travel agencies, and other ways of distribution in general. Making decisions in direct distribution requires an understanding of the economic variables that play a role in online distribution and online marketing in general. This means to be aware of and fully grasp the concept of online marketing mechanisms. However, it does not require deeper knowledge of the technicalities of the various forms of online marketing. Such technicalities are operative in nature, such as building tracking links for URLs used in a specific campaign, how to create an advertisement for search engines or how to set rich data markups on a website. These actions are best left to employees or agencies whom you contract in order to handle the nitty gritty of online marketing management.

Thus, I try to avoid digging deep into the technical details of online marketing. Technical aspects have been already elaborated on numerous times by very capable authors, mostly from fields outside the hotel industry. If you are interested in the technical details of setting up online marketing campaigns, I suggest turning to one of the many textbooks and online resources on the subject, which are available in abundance.

As for style, I tried to write his book in a non-scientific way, yet being precise and drawing on economic concepts whenever needed in order to present the full content of an idea. The content of this book should provide the reader with plausible and comprehensible facts about the big picture of online marketing in the hotel industry. Its attempt is not to deliver a fully-fledged scientific study, referencing numerous sources and indulging in complex formulas and citations. Rather, it attempts to display real-life management experience, without compromising the validity of its arguments by using lax terminology. Thus you will find few references. Some of the chapters in this book encompass numbers, formulas and ratios. These originate from my own experience in working on a diverse e-commerce portfolio of hotels, thus there are no references made to external sources.

1.2. Why Online Marketing for Hotels?

Hoteliers worldwide are confronted with an inevitable consequence of the internet economy: Its tendency to produce winner-takes-most markets has led to the build-up of an oligopolistic or quasi-monopolistic distribution landscape for selling hotel rooms. The situation today is that the online distribution of rates and rooms is dominated by online travel agencies (OTAs), who exert immense market power. This market power allows OTAs to command acceptance of high commissions for the bookings they generate, taking a big bite out of hotels' profitability and creating pressure on margins. The development from offline to online distribution has been steady in the tourism & hospitality industry ever since the first websites started selling rooms online. This resulted in a comparatively high centralization in online distribution for this industry today, where – depending on what region in the world you look at – two to three OTAs control the market for online hotel distribution. This oligopolistic structure naturally leads to a disparity in bargaining power, where even large hotel chains get the short end of the stick in commission negotiations with OTAs.

Of course, OTAs do have a legit business model: they consolidate hotel offerings into one platform and offer consumers a broad choice of hotels, thereby drastically reducing search costs for consumers. But also for hotels, OTAs (in principle) take on a valuable function, in that they take away from the hotel the need to worry about distribution. An OTA spends huge budgets on marketing, in order to attract users to its website, who will then eventually book a hotel. The hotel has no stake in the acquisition and conversion of bookers. Thus, the cost of acquisition - and its associated risk - is incurred exclusively by the OTA. The OTA has to convert the acquired users into bookers, this is her risk. For successfully converted users, that is, actual room bookings, the OTA then takes a fee for its services from the hotel (i.e. a commission). This is a comprehensible case for arguing that a hotel should leave distribution and marketing to external parties. And since today the majority of hotel rooms are booked online, this basically means leaving distribution to OTAs.

The problem is that the oligopolistic structure of the OTA market – with mostly duopolistic regional structures in most parts of the world – brings with it extreme bargaining power on the OTA side. In the long run this means that commission payments for hotels tend to increase, if hotels are not able to reduce their dependence on OTA distribution. On a broader level, this ultimately threatens the industry's already low profitability and even has the potential to bring some hotels to the verge of zero profitability. Worst-case scenario for some hotels will be the wipe-out: Because their room distribution is entirely depending on OTAs, it decreases their profit margins to the point where they are equal to or less than zero.

The responsible long-term oriented hotel operator should thus consequently look to diversify his distribution portfolio by adding more non-OTA bookings to it. Contemporary distribution brings with it that such a diversification must heavily rely on e-commerce, that is selling rooms via an own website online. Growing an e-commerce business requires that one understands fully the way that online distribution and online marketing work, and what levers one can pull in order to achieve the aforementioned distribution diversification. It is the aim of this book to provide its reader with such an understanding of hotel online marketing, thereby giving him the skills to flexibly design the most effective strategy in order to gain more independence from OTAs, reduce commission payments, and enjoy healthy margins.

If there is one word to describe the underlying paradigm of this book, it is *efficiency*. Almost all of the marketing measures presented here can have a place in a hotel's marketing strategy, however, it is the right dosage of each and mix that decides about whether your advertising spend gives you the maximum return. This is why any of the material presented in this book is analyzed according to question: *What's the return?*

1.3. Basic Definitions and Starting Points

Throughout the study of this book you will encounter a limited amount of specific online marketing lingo. Although I tried to keep the use of such professional language to a minimum for reasons of accessibility, there are some basic concepts that are elemental for the reader to internalize. These terms are explained below, familiarizing with them will help you navigate throughout this book:

Advertiser: The party creating and placing an advertisement. In our case: you, the hotelier.

Ad Spend: The funds that are allocated towards a certain online marketing channel or single campaign, i.e. the money spend on online advertisements.

Publisher: A party offering to place advertisements on its websites. In principle, this can be any type of website that is willing to display advertisements in various formats.

Cost-per-Click (CPC): The predominant form of reimbursement in online marketing. For every click on an advertisement, the publisher (i.e. provider of online advertisement space) is paid a certain amount of money by an advertiser (i.e. the advertising brand, or hotel in our case)

Cost-per-Order (CPO): Traditionally a form of reimbursement on a per-order-basis, or in the case of hotels, on a per-booking-basis. For every order that an advertiser realizes via a publisher, the publisher is paid a percentage of the order value or a fixed amount for each booking.

Cost-of-Sale (COS): Like CPO, the cost-of-sale is the ratio of cost over revenue. However, the expression COS is used in a different context, where CPO does not satisfy the requirement for contextual accuracy. The COS does not represent a reimbursement-model in online marketing, but rather represents a key-performance-indicator (KPI) required for efficiency-based management of online marketing channels. As will be explained in later chapters, this KPI serves a valuable function when comparing direct booking (or website) performance with commissions of online travel agencies. COS is the most important concept for managing online marketing. If you are to remember just one concept from this book, it should be this one.

Cost-per-mille (CPM): Is the classical form of reimbursement in display marketing or any format that thrives on the number of people *seeing* an ad, as opposed to clicking on it. It principally denotes the amount of money an advertiser pays to have a thousand views on his advertisement.

Direct Booking: A booking that comes from a hotel's own website.

Pull-marketing and Push-marketing: In order to formulate an exhaustive online marketing strategy, it is important to separate between push and pull marketing. While the former refers to marketing measures that try to push a product into the market, that is *create demand* in the first place, the latter aims at *tapping into active demand, which means consumers actively searching* for product offerings that match their respective need, and then converting this interest. This differentiation is useful when carving out the different positions that certain online marketing channels can have in an overall strategy. For example, search engines are a classic form of pull-marketing, whereas Email-Marketing is a typical push-channel.

Return on Ad Spend (ROAS): Technically, this is just the inverse value of the COS, but in context it is more useful to describe the return that you get when spending one monetary unit on online advertising. For example, an ROAS of 10 means that you get 10 units of revenue for each monetary unit you put into advertising. As opposed to COS, ROAS is usually expressed as an absolute number, i.e. as a multiplier of ad spend.

Traffic: Generally, traffic in the context of online marketing denotes the users active on a particular website.

Traffic can be interpreted by measuring in clicks, time spent on website and the number of webpages visited (also called pageviews). For the purpose of this book, traffic will be used to describe the amount of visitors (sometimes also called "users") coming to your website. As a rule of thumb, more traffic is better; however, there are dimensions of quality attached to traffic. That means for particular types of traffic, more is not always better, because the type of traffic acquired is not valuable. E.g. website visitors with virtually no interest in buying on a website are low quality, and having more of them does not add value to the website.

Besides these definitions, a number of assumptions are made about factors which play a role in designing an effective online marketing strategy. The following list shows those elements. These are not directly part of online marketing, but still decisive in the overall success of your strategy: They represent the *ceteris paribus conditions of your online marketing strategy*. Given the target audience of this book, I presume that you, the inclined reader, are familiar with the concepts listed below:

> > **A state-of-the-art website**: Without a state-of-the-art website, even the most carefully crafted marketing strategy will run into a dead end. Usability standards, full responsiveness to device types such as mobile phones and tablets, and

website loading speed are indispensable preconditions.

> **Basic elements of content**: Up-to-date picture material, relevant descriptions and copywriting are assumed to be existent. Without such basics, you do not need to think about online marketing in the strategic sense.
> **Systems**: Technical features such accurately working interfaces between website, internet booking engine (IBE) and central reservation system (CRS) and/or property management system (PMS), relevant e-mailing-software and website tracking systems are must-haves.
> **Tracking and reporting**: Constant monitoring of campaign success is of the essence. Therefore, you need accurate tracking tools and people that are able to use them, reporting the success of your campaigns back to you. These can by your own employees, or agency partners you are working with.

In short, these four very basic hygiene factors of e-commerce are assumed to be in place and working. Otherwise, any type of marketing will crackle if your setup does not meet these requirements and you will not be able to capitalize fully on your direct booking potential.

If you feel that some of these requirements are not yet met in your setup, you should make sure that they are taken care of first, before you start laying out investment plans for online marketing. Literature on these factors is abundant and dealing with them would go beyond the scope of this book, as it tries to provide a guide for generating more direct bookings for those who have already mastered the basic groundwork for of an online presence for a hotel, not explain the very fundamental aspects of e-commerce in general. Taking this as a given provides the starting point for our digression into the world of online marketing for hotels, developing the understanding about its mechanisms and how you can make them best work for you.

The remainder of the book is structured as follows: In chapter 2 the various online marketing channels are presented. Each channel follows the common notation of online marketing for that specific channel, presents the basic economic model and the mechanisms behind and dives into the pros and cons from the perspective of a hotel advertiser.

Chapter 3 then takes a closer look at some very common and hyped-up marketing subjects and tries to put them into perspective. Their role in a sustainable online marketing strategy is limited, because they have a tendency to turn into cash burners with very limited effect on revenue and sales.

Following, chapter 4 takes on the task of making sense of the presented marketing channels in a holistic way. Here, you will learn about concepts that allow you to make use of the measures presented in chapter 2 in the most effective way. You will learn about the concepts that separate a "good" online marketing from one that is concerted, sustainable and competitive edge. Chapter 5 sums up and describes how to formulate strategy from the insights gained through this book.

2. Online Marketing - The Hotelier's Choice

2.1. Effective but Expensive: Metasearch

The term "Meta" has become one of the buzzwords in hotel and travel distribution. Granted, the growth of so called metasearch engines[1] has been impressive and the recent move of Google pushing its hotel-ads product hints that this is indeed one important line of distribution that is here to stay. Proving to be an opportunity to find relief from growing OTA commissions and generate direct bookings, metasearch engines have by now come to a level of significance that is begging the question of whether they really constitute a more efficient and less costly way of selling hotel rooms. Or, whether they are just a new form of online distribution that still exhibits the inherent feature of few-to-many marketplaces, where few dictate prices to many, i.e. the hotels, thus creating just another string of dependency in hotel distribution.

---

[1] Examples of which are websites like Trivago, Tripadvisor or Kayak, to name a few.

To answer this question, we have to immerse into the business model of metasearches. Precluding, it is obvious that from a technical viewpoint alone, metasearches show potential for creating independence from OTAs. However, the journey to realizing this potential is not without pitfalls and not knowing or disregarding them may lead to quite frustrating – and costly – experiences with metasearch marketing.

In order to skim the full sales potential from metasearch, you first have to understand what a metasearch engine is and what type of business model it follows.

The basic function of a metasearch is to compare prices. It does so by feeding in prices from a) OTAs and b) Brand Name travel business, such as hotels, airlines, tour operators. It displays all the prices for a particular product, say a hotel room, with the requested parameters such as dates and room occupancy behind. Once a user clicks on the price, he is redirected to the website of the seller, e.g. the OTA or hotel chain.

The metasearch business model

The business model of a Metasearch is quite simple: Charge the advertiser each click that produces a redirect to his website. Thus, a metasearch sells clicks and it usually sells to the highest bidder. As a result of having many bidders in an auction for, say, a search for a hotel room for 2 persons for 1 night in Milan on December 1st, the metasearch creates a ranking, in which these bidders, i.e. the advertisers are presented and the screen of the user who put in the request.[2] As an advertiser bidding, you will rank a) in comparison to other hotels and b) for that particular hotel in comparison to other advertiser who sell (your) hotel, such as OTAs.

Hence, we have a simple CPC model that each metasearch follows, usually enriched by a so called quality factor. A quality factor is usually a well-kept black box that a metasearch uses in addition to the level of CPC bids to determine ranking, arguably with complex algorithms behind. One would expect that the lower the advertisers room rate (I will also refer to rate as price, the two are used interchangeably), the higher he ranks in comparison to sellers as well as other hotels. There can be other factors influencing ranking, such as reviews and content quality on that particular meta, but the two most important influencers of your ranking will be CPC bid and price.

---

[2] A request – for the purpose of this book – denotes any parameter combination of travel date, number of rooms, destination, length of stay and number of persons traveling, entered by a user on that metasearch website and transmitted from the metasearch to the respective advertiser, e.g. a certain hotel chain.

Between the two, CPC is most likely the dominant ranking determinant, because it makes sense businesswise for metas to allow for higher rankings through higher bids: It is the incentive compatible factor in the meta business model. More clicks on high CPC bids makes the meta pocket more money. Hence, it makes sense for a meta to reward high bidders by placing the bidder high up in the ranking. Wait a minute you say, what about the advertisers room price? Should not the best room price/rate be the most important determinant for ranking? Well, yes and no. Yes, because users obviously go on price comparison engines to compare prices and they expect to find the best price there. A meta that would structure its ranking exclusively or predominantly on CPC bids would exhibit random price structures at best. Users would realize over time that they do not get a transparent price comparison via that meta, ultimately abandoning its future use.

However, in the metasearch business model, revenue is maximized by increasing the number of clicks on its advertisements and the price level of the average click (i.e. CPC), which forces metasearch engines to put strong emphasis on the CPC bid in order to determine the ranking of advertisers. Thus, it makes sense for a meta to have a user click on an offer that ranks on the top position (which users will intuitively do), come back, look at other prices further down the list and click again, and possibly again. Keep in mind that once the user has clicked, the meta is out, it does not primarily care whether the user converts or not. So it makes sense to rather use a model that rewards high CPC bidding instead of rewarding having the best price. This is why you sometimes find the best price available not being displayed at all, because the CPC of the seller is simply too low. Displaying results solely on the basis of best price would befuddle the metas algorithm and endanger revenue maximization. Hence, it makes sense for a metasearch to show users the best price just about enough to keep their image of best-price-visibility, but still put emphasis on rewarding high CPC bidding. Given the competitive auction design behind the advertiser-bid-model, it can be stated that the incentive structure in the metasearch business model tends to lead to comparatively high CPCs for advertisers.

The metasearch success variables
We can now derive the factors that make the meta business model thrive, thereby understanding what it means for you as a hotel advertiser and your online marketing strategy.

Consider the following list of parameters, which is applicable to any advertising and bidding on metasearch.

These four elements will decide about the performance that you are able to achieve in metasearch marketing:

> Average Price level of your website
> Price-structure and differentials of your distribution landscape as a whole (own website, OTAs, wholesale rates, tour operators)
> Your website's conversion rate
> Maximum willing-to-pay commission (i.e. COS) for bookings on own website

I will now turn to the first case where we apply the above defined concept of cost-of-sale, or COS. Using it will allow you to determine the average level CPC around which you should structure your bids on metasearch engines.

The first thing you have to do in order to determine this level, is to set a maximum COS that you are willing to incur per booking. Set this as your fixed variable, say 15% per booking. You have to know what your average conversion rate on that particular metasearch engine is and the average booking value, then you can determine how many clicks you are able to internalize at any CPC for one booking. Thus, you can determine the maximum CPC that you are willing to pay with these input variables.

Determining Your Bids on Metasearch

① $\text{COS} = \dfrac{\text{CPC} \times \text{Clicks} \times \text{Conversion Rate}}{\text{Booking Value}}$

...solve for CPC...

② $\text{CPC} = \dfrac{\text{COS} \times \text{Booking Value}}{\text{Clicks} \times \text{Conversion Rate}}$

⟶ This gives you the maximum bid

Controlling the variables

If you are advertising on metasearch, you will find that users will click on your ads, even if you do not have the best price, or rank on position one. However, odds are that they will not convert. This is the online version of window shopping – users will go to your website, maybe view its content and the nice happy talk you provide, but ultimately buying where it is cheapest (and available, of course). This means that you must carefully control the most important variable that determines the outcome of your bidding strategy, in order to realize the maximum conversion potential that the given metasearch provides: price, price and price again:

> You have static net wholesale rates active? I suggest you shut those down before going in the meta business. Wholesale rates cannot be controlled [effectively] and are likely to pop up just about anywhere on the internet. Do not be surprised if you are beaten by 20% or more percent on your gross direct selling price by yourdubiousotafromsomeplaceunknown.com on a metasearch.

> For chains only: Do single hotels have the power to contract own rates with OTAs and do so on a frequent basis? Odds are that you will find these deal-rates on metasearch. You should then either make sure your own website also has these rates or take away the power from hotels to design such deals (without your knowledge). Few things are more dragging than finding out about some OTA beating your website price by x, simply because a deal with an OTA has gone unnoticed.

> The average rate (or shopping basket, to use e-commerce terminology) determines how many clicks you can incur before for any given level of COS? If it is small, you will need an extremely high conversion rate. Vice versa, if it is large, you

can afford to buy a lot of clicks before making one conversion. The lower your average rate, the less likely it will be to scale metasearch beyond a very small level. This is due to the asymmetric relation between CPC bids and price level variance for all hotels on a particular request. That is, the CPC levels are the same for all bidders, regardless of whether they sell a room at 50 or 100. Given a similar maximum COS that each is willing to realize, the hotel with the price at 50 will not be able to internalize as many clicks as the hotel at 100 at any given CPC. This is why metasearch bidding for 5-star hotels is much more likely to provide an adequate return than for 2-star hotels: Their average revenue per booking simply allows them to pay for a high number of clicks before having to generate a conversion. Other than that, there are of course the usual conversion drivers that will determine whether your metasearch strategy will turn out to be a success, such as usability and website performance, product quality, brand name, positive reviews and content quality.

The cost intensity of metasearch

Be aware that you will always compete with OTAs on Metasearches. OTAs inevitably have an advantage in generating returns from non-brand[3] searches on metas. These account for the predominant share of requests done on metasearches. Competition is fierce and CPCs on popular locations have a tendency to reach absurd levels.

Realize that essentially, what metasearches do is to buy traffic via performance marketing from the supply side and sell that traffic with a mark-up to the demand side, i.e. hotels and OTAs. This is what I call traffic arbitrage. That is, they buy traffic and sell it via cost-per-click at a higher price to hotel websites and OTAs. Hence, the prices that metasearches charge and will charge in the future are strongly positively correlated to the cost of performance marketing – in particular on search engines. Odds are that the prices of search engine marketing will increase in the future due to the monopolistic structure of the search engine market, and hence prices – i.e. CPCs – on metasearches will increase accordingly. The dependency on Google and the according cost structure is also one of the reasons why metasearches constantly look for additional revenues and changes in their business models, alas, direct or instant book options where they charge commissions for, display advertising solutions or flat fees charged for information services such as display

---

[3] A non-brand search – or generic search – on a metasearch engine is search request purely on destination (e.g. "Frankfurt") as opposed to a brand search, where the hotel (brand) name is included

of telephone numbers or email-Links. Reason being, that they try to create more options of traffic monetization for themselves, thereby improving their gross margin for any given level of traffic acquisition.

This is why COS for Metasearch-Bookings is usually among the highest of your marketing channels. Nonetheless, they are also able to deliver visibility like no other marketing channel and allow hotel's websites to participate in their growth. In the long-run, this gives way to spill-over effects on SEO, SEA and direct traffic, allows you to collect Email-Opt-Ins and learn about guest preferences as you simply bring bookings away from OTAs to your own website. Although pricey, Metasearch should form a key element in your online marketing strategy. This is where consumer traffic is shifting to, and you should not leave the field to OTAs to seize this opportunity.

This is why metasearches are very expensive on cost-per-order level. Although their conversion rates are among the highest, the high CPCs make buying bookings on metasearches a costly endeavor. Nonetheless if you have your pricing in line than being visible on metasearches is a must, because otherwise you leave the field to the OTAs, who will be visible on metasearches (at least their own). From a strategic viewpoint, you will rather incur high COS on metasearches in order to shift business to your own website and prevent OTAs from growing their share in your distribution mix, which will ultimately give them greater bargaining power in the future and the power to enforce higher commission levels. Metasearch marketing thus has a highly strategic component attached and one should always value the strategic benefit of bargaining power and the opportunity to gather user data over keeping short term cost-per-order levels low at any price.

This is why I believe metasearches to be an indispensable part of any long term marketing strategy, as they are providing immense scalability potential to your brand.com website distribution. metasearches are here to stay. The trend that they take up a higher share in visibility of hotel searches will maintain at least for the foreseeable future. Critical voices bemoan that this development simply means that dependency on OTAs is shifted to a dependency on metasearches. However, I believe that this trend can nonetheless be exploited by hotels. Because unlike OTAs, metasearches give hotels the opportunity to extricate brand visibility and customer data from their listings. So although the price per booking may on some Meta be comparable to the level of OTA commissions - around 20-25% - the costs of Metasearch bookings have a medium to long term investment dimension attached to them that is completely absent in OTA bookings.

2.2. A Marketer's Favorite: Search Engine Marketing

Paid search result advertisement is by many considered the holy grail of online marketing in travel, and hotel distribution in particular. Indeed, next to organic search results, paid online search advertisements – or search engine marketing (SEM) – on Google, Bing, Yahoo and the like are the primary source for website traffic to most online sellers of travel services, and there is little evidence that this will change in the near future.

The reason for this can be found in the simple fact that almost any online hotel booking involves some form of "research" on a search engine by the booker.

This implies that that search engine results are an important source of visibility for websites, making it essential for any successful direct booking strategy to integrate search engine marketing.

How SEM works

The basic mechanism of SEM works as follows: You bid on a certain keyword along with other bidders who are equally, less or more interested in bidding on this keyword. Every bidder has the intention of bringing traffic to his website by collecting clicks on his SEM ads. The monetary value that the bidder attributes to a click on this keyword will determine the maximum CPC that he is willing to pay. The search engine provider (e.g. Google) now collects all bids and determines the winning bidder, second, third and so on, and displays their ads on the respective place on their search engine result page. In addition to the CPC, a so called quality factor is taken into account to determine the ranking. The quality factor is a sort of black box, whose formula behind is known only to the search engine. Of course, there are identifiable variables such as click-through rate, ad quality etc., but the exact algorithm is kept secret. For our purposes, it suffices to know that this quality factor exists, and that the optimization of these variables playing into it must be taken into account, but is rather part of everyday management than an explicit part of strategy, and hence, not of the issue at this point.

Two types of SEM

SEM by its nature allows create high levels of visibility for one's website. However, visibility does not imply revenue generated. Because a) one has to skim clicks from this visibility and b) convert these clicks into bookings. Thus, in order to take advantage of the opportunities that SEM opens up in an economically sensible way, one has to firmly understand the operating mode of the two most basic classes of SEM-keywords: brand and generic[4]. The

---

[4] The term "keyword" always denotes a search term of some sort, regardless of whether it is just a single word or a combination of two

former refers to a word or combination of words - i.e. a phrase - that contains a trademark of some sort. For example, your hotel brand name, such as Hotel Palais xyz. The latter refers to phrases that lack such trademark, such as "hotel in Paris" or "book hotel Copenhagen". The two classes – with regard to your online sales strategy – are to be distinguished on two levels: search volume and intention.

Search volume refers to the number of searches that are performed on a particular keyword. It just so happens that in travel, generic searches outmatch brand searches for any specified location by far. This is due to the commodity nature of the hotel product: Usually, buying frequency is low and brand attachment is less important than quality and price. From this, it follows that the majority of searches done is based on generic keywords. E.g., the overall number of searches in a given time period for "hotel London" is significantly higher than for "London Hilton Hotel". By **intention** I refer to whether or not a user has the dimension "brand" in mind when doing a search. That is, keywords that include trademarks or brand terms inevitably imply that the user is looking either for one particular hotel or for a particular brand of hotels (usually in a specified location). Generic keyword searches lack this dimension. Here, users are probably

---

or more words.

certain about the location, but they have either no brand name hotel in mind or do not care about the brand of the hotel they will stay in.

Now assume that the following causal relationship is true: more traffic means more bookings, and more bookings mean more revenue, and assume that each bidder tries to maximize revenue. It should follow that there will be more and higher bids for keywords with high search volume, because each bidder wants to be visible on these keywords to get a piece of the pie. Now, to make this process even more competitive, the predominant part of searches concentrates on a small number of similarly structured search terms - the shorthead of keyword searches, e.g. "hotel Frankfurt" or "hotels in Frankfurt", as illustrated in Figure 1. Inevitably, you will find the highest CPCs on generic, shorthead keywords.

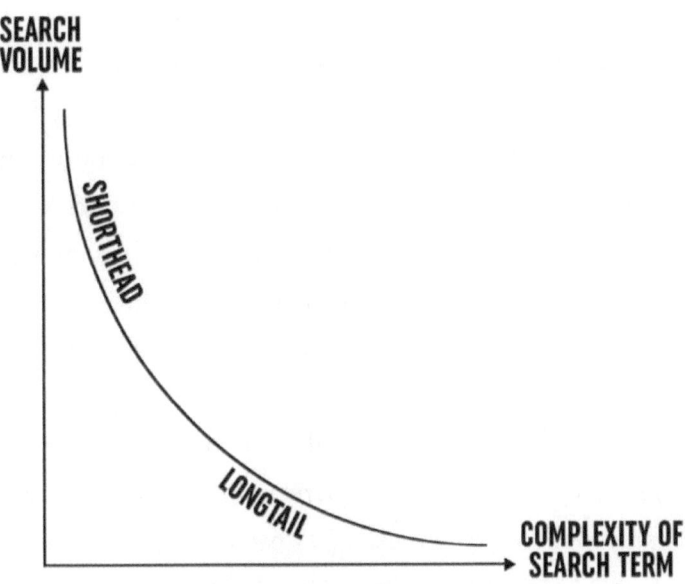

Figure 1 - Shorthead and Longtail Keywords

However, CPCs are only half the story. Because the user typing in a generic search term is not your much desired brand aficionado, the conversion rates for generic search traffic are chronically low. The users that you attract with short head keywords usually are price sensitive, expect to choose among many options and rank low on any type of brand loyalty. Low conversion rates imply that one must generate a comparatively large number of clicks in order to generate a booking, hence overall costs per booking are high.

However, there is still a chance for you to thrive on bids for generic keywords, in what is called the "long tail". Long tail denotes keywords that are generic, yet low in search volume. Such keywords usually include a higher count of words and refer to very specific queries targeted to a certain event or micro-location. For example, the search term "hotel close to main station in Amsterdam" targets a small radius around the main station in Amsterdam, at least this is what one can expect the user to have in mind. The number of hotels that are really relevant for this search query is much smaller than the total number of hotels in Amsterdam. Assuming your hotel is located directly next to the main station, it might be attractive for you to bid on this keyword, as you are now a) catering directly to the request of the user and b) face less competition from the OTA side, because in the proximity of the main station, there might only be 5 hotels (listed on the OTAs).

Thus, the conversion potential on the basis of mere availability of hotel rooms is corrected in favor of the single hotel. We see that the cost per order ratio will be more likely to be acceptable for the hotel, as it now converts more clicks, given that its offerings provide a high fit to the search intention of users that are looking for a "hotel close to main station in Amsterdam".

The second part of a strategy for long tail generic keywords is to look for keywords that re low-search-volume, can but have high-impact when producing a sale. These keywords encompass a narrowly defined interested, but with a high level impact on your revenue. For instance, suites or multi-room/multi-night-bookings are at comparatively high price points. If a hotel product is designed to cater to such special interests (for example, high net worth business clients from overseas or group bookings for special events), it will be worthwhile to test whether you can generate a sufficient ROAS on the long tail of these special interests. Given that booking value is usually way above average, you will also be able to operate on a high CPC / Low-Conversion-Rate-ratio. In such cases, generic SEM will be successful if you bid high selected keywords that describe a narrow niche in which your hotel owns a competitive edge. In most cases, this will be your location or the surroundings of your location. If you can't find that niche, I suggest you stay out of the bidding on generic keywords altogether.

Aside from generic keywords, there are of course brand keywords that you should use. Even more, you should make bidding on your brand keywords the top priority in your SEM strategy. Reason being that in no form of search, the intention of the user is higher. Searching for a particular hotel name or hotel brand in a particular destination clearly shows a very high level of interest for that particular hotel. That is, the degree of congruence between what the user is actually looking for and what you have to offer is extremely high. Naturally, the conversion potential of such a user is also comparatively high and hence the revenue extraction potential. Bidding on your hotel name – and combinations thereof – is hence paramount to generating adequate return on marketing spending.

In either case of search engine marketing – brand or generic keyword bidding – the potential for traffic and revenue generation is highest in this form of online marketing, because of the adamant position of search in the customer journey and the quasi-monopolistic position of search engine providers. Simply put, (almost) everyone will visit Google when looking to book a hotel online.

2.3. The Trump Card: Search Engine Optimization

The SEO mechanism

Managing search engine optimization (SEO) is very similar to the game of SEM, with the simple but important twist that its effects are more long term and it is *much* cheaper than SEM - if done right. The main difference between the two is that in SEM you pay the search engine on a click-basis for displaying an advertisement high on a search result page. In SEO you try to achieve such a high ranking *organically*, through adapting certain parts of your website so the search engine is able to better judge why it is relevant for particular search queries.

For any type of search query the attention paid to a website – i.e. the number of clicks it receives – decreases significantly with the number of ranks it is behind the top position for that particular search query. Page one of the search engine result pages (SERPs) is where the action is, page two will attract some patient users with too much time on their hands, and once you arrive on pages three, four and beyond, the party is basically over. Your ranking will directly translate into the amount of traffic you will get out of specific keywords and search phrases. Hence, a high ranking will bring you more traffic. It follows, that SEO denotes all that aim at improving one's position on search engine result pages (SERPs). In other words: SEO boils down to "trying get to the top spot on Google and Bing".

Generally, non-paid, "organic" search results are ranked according to the relevance that the search engine attributes to a website in relation to a specific search phrase, also called "keyword". For instance, the search phrase "5star hotel Madrid" will return numerous links to websites on Google, and the ranking of these websites is based on what Google thinks is the best match to this search phrase. The exact algorithm Google employs to determine the order of organic search results is – for the most part – a black box. However, the general agreement among SEO-experts as to how search engine algorithms work is that they scan websites for so-called *signals*, which are then interpreted according to a predefined rule, which eventually determines the position of a website amongst others (in relation to a given search phrase). Although you can find long lists of signals in books on SEO and websites, which are readily available, regularly updated and published, the actual algorithm remains – for obvious reasons[5] – unknown to the public.

As the list of signals is extensive and their micro-optimization requires profound knowledge of SEO, this

---

[5] Obviously, the core competency - and hence business model - of a search engine is its search algorithm.

task is best left to your SEO-Manager or web agency.[6] For our purpose of strategy formulation, it suffices to understand that the most relevant signals in one way or another relate to the *content* of your website. That is, the information you provide on your website (in written or media form) and its reference to respective keywords (i.e. linkages).

Understand that the beauty of SEO is that you get can quite far by polishing up your website's content, which does not require heavy marketing investments. Simply provide content that is relevant and you will see your website climbing the SERP ladder. Since content is relevant when it matches keywords, you will want to make sure that contents match those keywords that you expect to denote what your hotel actually has to offer.

SEO in online marketing strategy
Strategically, you face a similar situation in SEO as you do in SEM: Generic keywords are highly competitive. That is, many players, such as OTAs, other hotels, tour operators and basically any website trying to sell hotel rooms online, try to optimize for the short head of hotel searches, e.g. "hotels in Berlin". For these keywords,

---

[6] You will find numerous SEO-Experts offering you their services on the web. What they basically do is to try and make your websites signals shine more brightly, so that search engines will judge your website to be more relevant.

single hotels and even hotel chains face high barriers when trying to optimize towards higher rankings because of the supply asymmetry between Hotels and OTAs. The latter being at an extreme advantage, as their massive inventory tends to be ranked very high by search engines. Huge inventories bring with them an abundance of content and linkages, which Google tends to weigh comparatively high. A single hotel, but even large hotel chains are not able to match these inventories on any given destination. Try it out for yourself - compare the ranking of the biggest hotel group that comes to your mind with the ranking of an OTA on a search like "hotel destination xyz" and then compare the number of hotels they offer in that particular destination.

However, your brand or hotel name and a long tail of very specific keywords and phrases that generate only comparatively low search volumes open up opportunities for hotels.

Recall the intention of any performed search – if a brand name is involved, the probability of converting a user into a booker increases significantly, so you want to get a hold on as many of these brand searches as possible. Being the owner of your brand, you have certain advantages in brand SEO. Domain name, relevant content and a logical and well denoted link structure of your website are signals that are certain to be major influencers on ranking. As your brand is by definition an image of your hotel (or your services) the optimization of the above mentioned SEO (hygiene) factors is easier for you than for others. Whereby "easier" means: the focus of your website on your brand implies that signals from your website are attributed more relevance by search engines in relation to a certain search phrase.

Things become a little more sophisticated with generic keywords. As you want to target the long tail without the support of your brand, creating relevant content becomes more challenging, because a) you have to find keywords that actually match what your hotels is offering and b) those keywords have to generate traffic volumes at levels that actually contribute a meaningful share to overall revenue to justify investment (in content creation, or copywriting).
It follows that you have to find keywords that will either allow for a *steady flow of bookings at average value* or by finding *low-demand but high-impact niche* keywords that lead to few bookings of extraordinary high value.

The *first case* represents combinations of high volume keywords, such as in combination with m*edium to low search volume keywords*.

E.g.:

> hotel Berlin (high search volume)
> + design (medium search volume)
> + spree river (low search volume)
> = "design hotel Berlin on spree river"

The *second case* combines *high to medium volume* keywords with keywords of *very low search* volumes,

E.g.:

> hotel London (high search volume)
> +Luxury SPA (low search volume)
> + girlfriends' treatment (very low search volume)
> = Luxury Spa hotel London girlfriends' treatment

In the first case, it can be anticipated that you will get a booking request from Joe average, but with a very specific search intention, i.e. a design hotel at river Spree in Berlin. The second case is even more specific and likely to not generate much traffic at all, but if your hotel caters to the interest of the user - in our case a particular spa offer for two or more females who may want to enjoy a day off together - the probability is high that this will be a high-value booking, because the request will most likely include multiple rooms and cross-sell revenue (e.g. SPA treatments).[7]

---

[7] As a basic rule for content on your website, you should provide exhaustive text and media not only on your hotel and all of its

To conclude, a note on design, the downside and future of SEO:

It is of utmost importance that your content is authentic. Users can tell the difference between genuine information and happy marketing talk. Keep in mind that your content does not only have to convince Google, but once the user is on your website, it has to convince him, too.

The main downside of SEO is that it takes comparatively long to exert its effects. SEO takes time because for the combination of signals to be recognized and ranked, the bots of search engines will need to visit your website continuously and often. Hence, it is not uncommon to see weeks or even months pass between an update of your website (e.g. a new text) and any impact on the SERP ranking. However, this delay between action and result is acceptable considering the upside that results from the combination the two dominant SEO-characteristics:

> low investment - high return ratio
> sustainable impact on traffic and revenue

---

amenities, but also on the surrounding area, things to do, surroundings, events (recurring, ongoing or permanent) or other services you offer.

Considering that keyword search will be the most important traffic source for your hotel's website, I advise to think of it as an integral part of your hotel branding strategy.[8]

You might have realized by now that I consider SEO an integral part of any online marketing strategy. However, I am afraid the future of SEO does not look that bright: It becomes ever more apparent that search engines will monetize their traffic at the expense of organic search results. First-page search results are plastered with paid-for-advertising, which is particularly relevant for mobile traffic. To reach organic search results, a user has to perform 4-5 swipes down, depending on display size. In the long run, the consequence will be that overall visibility of organic search results decreases. Hence, this comparatively cheap source of traffic will provide a smaller share of traffic and bookings/revenue to your overall website revenue, which, unfortunately, tends to increase the average cost-per-order of your direct bookings overall.

---

[8] I would even go so far as to say that a significant competitive advantage opens up for those who develop a hotel name and hotel brand name with keyword search in mind. Cleverly combining specific generic keywords in your hotel's name will allow you to be found more easily and create a brand name that sticks in consumers' minds.

2.4. Mining for Gold: Social Media Marketing

Social media is probably the most hyped of all contemporary forms of online marketing, especially in the travel industry. The hype is reflected in an interminable number of agencies, consultants, marketers, websites and social media "experts" who constantly sing from the same hymn sheet: spend or die – those who do not heavily invest in social media will be wiped out soon, because social media will be the only relevant form of online marketing in the near future. Facebook, Twitter, Instagram, Pinterest, or Snapchat – platforms for engaging in social media as a means of marketing communication are abundant. Granted, the list of successful social media campaigns is long and there are companies that have thrived extremely well on social media marketing. However, the success examples are predominantly found in in the FMCG, fashion, and event industries, which is why I am hesitant to transfer the opportunities that social media opens up in theory, up onto the hotel industry. Social media marketing is rarely the gold mine of sales that it is often portrayed to be and before hastily starting ample investments in performance marketing and content on social media, one has to understand what it can do for hotels, and where its limits are.

The following paragraphs outline the basic mechanisms of social media marketing so as to help the reader to get a feeling for social media opportunities and what pitfalls to avoid.

In this context, it is first necessary to visualize that generally, the effects of any type of hotel marketing can unfold on two levels:

1. branding effects
2. bookings

Where for a hotel, the former ultimately is also only an indirect means to an end, that is, total bookings. To exhaustively distinguish the dimensions on which the two differ does not require deep analysis. While branding effects are for the most part *long term* and are usually not directly attributable to a specific campaign, effects on direct bookings are short term and can directly be attributed to a specific campaign, sales action or budget.

The problem with the return on investments in branding is that they are hard to quantify. In particular for the short term, this puts branding at a disadvantage, as there is usually no satisfying direct sales return attached to them. Thus, when competing for the allocation of budgets, funds go to other channels where sales are produced directly, and often rightfully so. Social media is generally more of the branding type and this chapter will explain why when it comes to allocating funds to social media campaigns, you should be extra careful.

The first step towards assessing the possible impact of social media, one must understand its two basic mechanisms: *content production* and *media advertising*.

By content production I refer to the original motive of all social media: Posts of pictures, videos, text or any combination thereof that engage some kind of response from users. Although each social media channel has a variety of names and functional descriptions, such as fans, likes, shares and the like, it suffices for strategic purposes to summarize these responses under "engagement". The result of such engagement can be referred to as organic reach. It denotes the number of people who interact via the social media channel with you. It is "organic" because you achieve such engagement without spending money on marketing this content.

The second mechanism of social media is media advertising. While it may be used to directly promote reach (i.e. content), its main purpose is to create visibility for advertisements that are intended to create clicks, and possibly bookings, on your website.

When used for content promotion, it supports the reach of your content by simply showing your content to users who belong to a predefined group assumingly in favor of your product or brand. You thus create visibility for your content beyond the pure organic reach, about which you usually have little control.

On the other hand, almost all social media channels are now open for commercial interests and you can use a variety of advertisement formats on social media channels. These are detached from content production, as for example display ads shown to users on Facebook. Be aware, that both mechanisms are able to feed of each other and create synergies.[9]

Social media content

You should look at social media through the 80/20 glasses: 20% of your social media channels – and on those, 20% of the content you produce - will create 80% of user response, or engagement. Unless you are severely overstaffed with personnel that knows how to run social media (which most likely you are not), my advice is to concentrate your social media efforts on one or two channels that are most intensely used among your target audience.

Aside from the functional difference of these two mechanisms, there is a third aspect to social media, which is related to its strategic use. Most individuals who use social media do so because of non-commercial reasons. That is, they want to interact with other individuals or –

---

[9] The details of display marketing follow in a later chapter and are for reasons of redundancy omitted here.

what is nowadays probably the main driver – to simply express their views, emotions, or look for attention from others. As a company, you face the challenge of entering this world on the basis of commercial interest. Thus you have to create content that manages to walk the fine line between helping your commercial interest and turning off users because of its overly visible marketing face.

To generate such content is indeed a non-trivial task and your options are highly predetermined by the type of hotel that you are running. As a general rule, the more services you offer in addition to the core service (i.e. a hotel bed), the more variation in engagement you will be able to extract from social media. Examples of such ancillary services are spa & wellness, restaurant, bar, gym and meeting rooms.

Creating content from these is vital to your social media strategy. You have a three star chef or Michelin guide cuisine? Your SPA offers exclusive exotic beauty treatments? Your gym features the last get-fit equipment and gives visitors a terrific view over the skyline? You offer an exotic range of cocktails? Talk about it! Any type of content that you can extract from additional services is useful. Also proven to work is to give your hotel a human face. Spa managers, Restaurant chefs or directors telling stories makes content more credible and attaches a value certificate to your content. In addition, a human face makes your brand or hotel look more approachable and hospitable. Whatever your ideas on content for social media are: Create it, publish it and see what creates the most attention and interaction, and then do it again. Using a continuously iterative process in the creation of social media content helps you identify what works best.

Irrespective of the type of content you publish is the rule that continuity is the key to success: You must be able to produce and publish content regularly, the minimum is not less than once a week. Otherwise, your community will die. Fans and followers implicitly demand to be fed [useful] content regularly. If they do not get it, they tend to lose interest and engagement will decline – user attention is limited and competition for it is extremely intense.

One of the most important pieces of advice in social media marketing is to stick to no more than two to three channels. It is tempting to jump on the bandwagon of ever new social media formats due to fear of missing out. However, one should never just do something because everybody else does it, and this is particularly true for social media marketing. Planning, creating and posting content is time consuming and personnel-intensive. Thus, in principle, you would have to create new and exclusive content for every additional social media format.

The opposite approach of this is content scaling, i.e. using the same or at least similar content across all your social media simultaneously. Such a strategy makes sense if the audiences on the different channels are mutually exclusive. Differences among audiences which would make for such exclusiveness are basically

> Differences between countries – e.g. one social media channel is popular among internet users in the US while it plays almost no role in Germany and your customers are coming in equal shares from these markets – this is rarely the case, except for very large global hotel brands
> Differences between age groups – e.g. people younger than 20 tend to use Snapchat and Instagram instead of Facebook, while in the age groups above 30, use of these channels is negligible. Such differences between ages of target groups of social media formats actually exist, however, your customer target group will not spread across all age groups.

Aside from these criteria, there is no mutual exclusiveness among users of social media channels. This means that it does not make sense to duplicate content published on a channel onto another one, as you will reach the exact same audience.

I thus recommend sticking to one or two social media channels that you use for publishing original and (for the most part) exclusive content. Scale economies, engagement growth and your social media manager will thank you.

Measuring the effectiveness of social media content
Sensible measurement of the effectiveness of social media content does not try to measure direct bookings. The branding component of pure social content - that is, content without a sales offer behind - sets limits to the measurement of its impact. KPIs such as direct bookings or even revenue generated are two far away in the purchasing funnel to be measured at a meaningful scale. However, immediate response tells you whether the type of content you publish is at least positively "ingested". Thus, relevant social media KPIs in this regard are a) fan & follower development and b) their ratio of engagement – the number of likes, shares, retweets and the like over your total fans/followers.

Social media advertising
Besides plain content publishing, almost all social media platforms allow you to run paid advertising campaigns[10],

---

[10] More generally referred to as performance campaigns.

either in order to promote content and make it more visible to users or to market products and services directly. With regard to direct bookings, the latter is of interest, as it – theoretically – opens up opportunities to direct users from the social media platform onto your website, where they can be converted into bookers. Social media platforms have released and continue to release numerous features that aim at attracting advertisers into spending more money on their platform, in order to take advantage of this – supposedly – massive potential that their sheer number of users represents. So much for theory. Reality shows, that for hotel online marketing social media tends to be the weakest performance marketing. If you seek to drive direct bookings and achieve a reasonable ROAS of 3 or more on your marketing money, social media should be last on your list. Most social media performance campaigns tend to deliver returns at an ROAS of 2 or less, once traffic is scaled to a substantial dimension. In other words, you spend 50% of the revenue generated on the social media campaign, which is of course not economically viable.

Why is this case? The explanation for the chronically low performance of social media as a sales channel for hotels is given by the very purpose that social media actually serves, that is, to drive *social interaction (digitally) among individuals*. Recall what has been said on the intention of users above. The intention of someone who visits a social media platform is primarily and foremost to communicate with others and express him or herself. This intention drastically reduces the susceptibility to commercial advertising messages, as compared to, for example a search engine or metasearch. This means that any social media performance marketing is at risk of being fundamentally delivered at the *wrong time*. This seems counterintuitive, as social media usually has the most sophisticated options for formulating target groups, as the providers sit on massive amounts of personal data: likes, shares, groups, places visited etc. etc. This means that not only can you advertise to your fans and followers, who have already displayed their affinity to your brand, but to all types of audiences that you define, thereby increasing reach with unmatched precision. You should thus be able to drill down target groups to those who are most likely to book with you and achieve very good conversion rates on your website.

The fallacy of this argument is that it neglects the underlying limitations on scalability for hotels. Except for the very large hotel chains, the hotel supply side's offering is very limited: One hotel in one destination. Consider a large resort hotel in a nice but remote location, somewhere in the mountains. The hotel does not belong to a big brand or chain and ranks in the very upper end of the price range. Being a resort hotel, the largest target group is individuals traveling on leisure, hence a target group with a very low buying frequency. Now assume that this resort starts a social media advertising campaign in order to attract direct bookers to its website.

What we now have is a combination of the following factors that we would need to consider in order to drill down our target audience:

> High price and accordingly high purchase value (this already shrinks any target audience drastically; in particular younger audiences, who still comprise the majority of social media users)
> Generally very low buying frequency (which excludes to a large extent impulsive purchases)
> Very specific location (remote and in the mountains; this leads to further exclusion of all those who are principally not interested in remote hotels in the mountains)
> Lack of image support through a brand that is renowned among a large audience (increases the perceived risk of the purchase decision)

One would now have to find a target audience that combines all of the features that can be deduced from the above factors: high income, interest in the particular location, receptive to non-brand hotels, and currently "in the mood" to purchase a hotel stay. You will find that the actual size of the potential audience becomes quite small.

Combine this with the non-commercial intention that users have and the result will be a very low ROAS and conversion rate for the campaign.[11]

Of course, there is no rule without exception: Performance marketing targeting fans and followers with discounted deals and special rates. This can actually drive direct bookings with ROAS of 3 or higher. Fans/followers are for obvious reasons receptive to advertisements of the respective brand/hotel, and with special – or even exclusive – offers impulse purchases can be triggered among this target group. But, to derive any number of bookings from such an advertisement (campaign) requires you to have a very large fan base (e.g. not less than 5.000 Facebook fans) and/or the ability to reach very large custom audiences. In preparation to performance marketing, it is hence to necessary to build up a sustainable and loyal fan base first. The second step is then to target this following with discounted offerings. Performance marketing in social media more than all other channels requires constant trial-and-error. It is possible to discover a gold mine in one's fan base, but it also possible to let a lot of cash go to waste.

---

[11] Conversion rates of less than 0.5% are common for social media campaigns in travel.

A note on Social Media and customer care

In addition to brand marketing, social media is rightfully considered a tool for customer care. Taking requests and taking care of customer complaints is actually one of the most common use cases for social media.

You should, however, draw a distinct line between social media as a means of online marketing and social media as a means of customer care. The trivial, but important difference between the two is while the former seeks to gain momentum in acquiring new customers or bring old customers back, the latter is exclusively concerned with current customers. More specifically, customers that are currently on site or customers who have booked with you but not yet arrived, or customers who have finished their stay but who have outstanding services with a need for settlement (e.g. payment, loyalty program rewards, invoicing and the like).

2.5. A Dream of Efficiency: Email-Marketing

As opposed to search engine marketing, social media or metasearch, email-marketing tends to take a rank of lesser priority in many online marketing strategies. This is not without reason: email-marketing has a reputation for comparatively low conversion rates, which seem to make it less effective for advancing revenue. My experience is that, e.g., the overall average conversion rate for an upscale resort ist between 0.8 and 1.2 per cent, for a midscale business hotel between 2.5 and 5.0 per cent.[12] Email-marketing tends to return conversion rates around 0.5 to 2.0 per cent, where most campaigns are in the range of 0.5 - 1.0 per cent. When extremely aggressive pricing is included, you may be able to achieve conversion rates around 1.0 per cent.

The on average comparatively low conversion rate of email-marketing is rooted in two factors:

> *Abusive practices* – i.e. spamming – have made users weary of e-mails with commercial intentions. This has resulted in most e-mails not being read. Also, e-mail clients often follow algorithms that over time will shift your e-mails into the SPAM folder,

---

[12] Conversion rate (CR) is defined here as number of bookings overall / Total number of website users; i.e. CR = Bookings/Visits.

which means that they are not discovered by recipients. The sheer *amount of e-mails* an average person receives per day creates a massive overload. Hence, the probability of an individual advertising e-mail being read is very small.

> *Its push-marketing nature* and *attached limitation of visibility*, set by the size of the email distribution list. In combination, this creates a limit on revenue generation potential. The reason being that push marketing tries to create demand and is thus confronted with a higher barrier to purchase than pull marketing. Combined with a small distribution list, this creates a natural ceiling to revenue growth potential. Put in simple terms: A guest can only so often visit your hotel before she is oversaturated with your product. In particular leisure travel is affected by this: People have limited free time on their hand and travel maybe twice or three times a year for leisure. These factors restrict push marketing severely. Compared to commodity products like clothing or beauty care, conversion on travel products for push marketing is chronically low.

However, although the above statements are generally valid, there are also arguments making a case in favor of email marketing:

> *E-mail marketing eliminates the middleman.* No mediator is between you and your customer - no OTA, no search engine, no metasearch, no publisher of any sort. You control everything – the offers, the content and design, the discount on prices. Also, the trend of increasing mobile device use works in favor of email marketing, as the mobile device as a touchpoint for one's email client allows for constant and quick access. The direct contact to your customer/guest is invaluable, from a cost-per-order-perspective. Without having to incorporate traffic suppliers such as search engines or metasearch, a large email-database allows you to cost-effectively stimulate directly attributable revenue.

> *Email marketing does not cost much.* Sending out an e-mail costs almost nothing. You will incur a little fix cost for email software and one-time setup costs for the creation of templates and designs. Variable costs are the creation of content for each mailing and the cost-per-e-mail (which is minimal). Compared to any performance marketing channel, the accumulated cost of email marketing is negligible. Investment has to be made in building up an email database, e.g. by incentivizing signups on your website by offering

vouchers or other goodies. This is, however, an investment in the actual sense, as it is more sustainable than one-off spending in performance marketing, where you do not extract value from the spend beyond the immediate booking. Opposed to this, an e-mail address, or lead, can become an asset, if you manage to convert the user into a loyal guest over time.

> Leads, i.e. newsletter recipients in your database, come from people that are already in contact with your brand, and most likely will have a positive attitude towards your brand. This implies that over time, you will be able to generate a more or less loyal following. When your database grows, *revenue from e-mail marketing comes in the sheer mass of leads*, even if conversion rate remains low. Thus, email marketing can become a powerful direct booking over time, when leads are collected continuously. There is particular emphasis on the last factor - growing a high quality lead database is of the essence.

There are a number of ways to acquire email addresses, but the ones with most impact and from the viewpoint of data protection safest methods are the following:

1. Ask for the email of every hotel guest upon check-in on the registration form, or at other touch points such as SPA-forms or restaurant bills.
2. Ask for a sign-up at the time of booking on your website
3. Incentivize sign-ups on your website. An incentive could be, e.g. participation in a sweepstake, vouchers in any form (%-off, fixed sum, freebies such as breakfast), or access to exclusive membership-rates not available to the public
4. Get your social media following to sign up for your Newsletter[13]– Fans and followers already exhibit interest in your hotel/brand, asking them for their email-addresses is easy and they have a comparatively high willingness to give it to you

Another benefit of email marketing is that it allows you to efficiently *cross- and up-sell on existing bookings*. Reason being that existing bookings in many cases give you the email of a guest, which can be used to send pre-stay emails in

---

[13] And vice versa, get your newsletter recipients to become social media followers. By doing so, you create spillover effects that enhance your brand's visibility and ultimately drives brand loyalty in the long term.

order to offer e.g. upgrades, special offers on restaurants or wellness or even add-on products to a stay, such as rental cars or event tickets. In addition to mailing campaigns, you should take advantage of the opportunities around existing bookings. In particular emails in preparation of future stays, referred to as *pre-stay mailings,* give you the opportunity to create win-win situations for the guest and you. For the guest, this means getting all relevant information about his stay in a concise and exhaustive format and entering his personal contact information via dedicated landing pages, thus saving time upon check-in.

Email and content: Interaction without transaction
Guests who are willing to hand out their email address to a hotel obviously show a genuine interest in the hotel or the overarching brand. Practice shows that such guests are more receptive to added services, up- and cross-selling, and brand interaction overall. In order to further strengthen the attachment of such guests to a brand, *content mailings* can be a useful tool. Generally, content mailings are triggers intended to bring traffic to a website *without* carrying a direct sales intention. Recipients receive added value from the content of such a mailing in and of itself, in other words, from the *story told*. Storytelling aims at creating a positive image of a brand, thereby enhancing the recollection of a hotel's name in the mind of the

customer/guest, eventually creating a loyal brand following. Recall the types of content elaborated on in the previous chapter on social media: In principle, anything that you published on your social media channels may lend itself for content mailings. In that way, you use an additional channel to distribute content, which provides leverage to the brand-building effects of social media. Also, it allows creating a more sympathetic brand identity, because your email communication distinguishes itself from the usual hard-selling-emails of other brands that fill most inboxes.

For content mailings, the dictum trial-and-error becomes even more relevant than for the rest of online marketing. Not all stories are equally effective for all hotel types, differences are showing between resort and business hotels, budget and luxury segments, beach and city destinations, and so forth. Testing the effectiveness of a content mailing should rest on the observation and comparison of web metrics only, such as in clicks, bounce rates and time spend on website. Given the lack of sales intention, measuring bookings or direct revenue are in this case obsolete.

No effective email marketing without quality data
Email marketing creates direct customer contact for enriching the customer lifetime value or guests in a way

that no other marketing channel can. The most important precondition for successful email marketing is *exhaustive and correct data*. Without correct data to act upon, email marketing cannot unfold its effects. For any email campaign, exhaustive, clean and structured guest data is of the essence. Data has to be

- a) *correct* – e.g. up-to-date address, personal details, overall revenue generated, revenue according to segments (such as SPA, F&B etc.) and
- b) *exhaustive* in representing a guests interests and preferences, such as e.g. when he books, where he books, what time of year he likes to travel, whether he travels business or leisure, what's his favorite cuisine, does he travel with a partner etc.

To ensure the collection of correct and exhaustive data, you have three main levers at hand:

1. *Check-in:* A good way to steer data collection at the front desk, during the interaction between guest and front office employee is to set incentives for high data quality. For instance, you may reward employees by the number of data sets

with a predefined number of completed fields (in your PMS or CRM software).

2. *Pre-stay emails / pre-check-in*: Shift the burden of keeping guest data correct to the guest himself by having him enter his correct information before arrival. This can be elegantly done by sending pre-stay emails, asking the guest to fill out a registration form online in order to save time at check-in. Doing so is a win-win: You get correct data while the guest saves time at check-in.

3. *Accounts/Logins*: This solution is suited most for hotel chains, as account creation requires a scalable product range in order to be attractive to users. A personal login section on a website requires users to identify themselves and it enables you to collect personal data, which is kept up-to-date by guests themselves. Coupling certain benefits and incentives, such as a special rate or instant gratification bonuses (any form of free goodies), to a website account helps in having users take the additional step of account creation. With such account users, you build up a reliable and accurate database of your guests as they fill in information themselves, thereby reducing possible error sources. Furthermore, the overall time needed to collect the desired data is reduced.

Despite the benefits that correct and exhaustive data can have on email marketing (and online marketing more generally), guest data still is often an undervalued asset for hotels. Reason being that the focus of most hoteliers is on operations and the resulting primacy of operative processes above marketing and distribution processes. From an operative viewpoint, collecting and managing guest data may pose additional work: more software systems, additional processes (collecting, matching, cleaning, structuring data) and increased cost (investment of time and money). A short-term focus on these operative downsides of guest data collection may prevent acknowledgement of the value of (structured) guest data, which tends to show its benefits long term. Thus, when weighing the cost and benefits of investments in data collection, consider that not having access to structured and exhaustive guest data in the long term brings with it very high opportunity costs:

1. Missing out on revenue from cross-selling and up-selling
2. Losing customers on their future bookings to OTAs or other more costly distribution channels (or even worse: to other hotels)
3. Missing opportunities to interact with guests and show appreciation, which pays in on hotel brand value in the long run.

2.6. Good Bang for the Buck: Affiliate Marketing

The term affiliate marketing basically denotes a form of commission based sales agreement between two parties that affiliate in order to sell a product or service. For our purpose, an affiliate can be any type of website that has the ability to potentially promote your hotel, by placing an advertisement and linking it to your website. The party showing the ad on his website is referred to as the "publisher" while you – the guy with the product – are referred to as the "advertiser". The commercial agreement between the two is as follows: If a booking is generated via the link that the publisher provides on his website, he is rewarded a commission for that sale. To find publishers, you have the option of either joining so-called affiliate networks, which are marketplaces that match supply and demand of publishers and advertisers, or you go into direct cooperation with publishers bilaterally. While the first option provides reach, the second usually provides more quality. Technically speaking, that is all there is to affiliate marketing.

Of more interest than the technical mechanism of affiliate marketing is its strategic implication and how it differentiates itself from other forms of online marketing. Because, although technically affiliate marketing is as simple as placing ads on publisher websites and hence a very simple and quick-to-implement form of online marketing, it requires you be extremely aware of its effects in your overall online marketing mix. For any type of affiliate marketing, it is extremely important that you consider the following elements:

1. Hotel pricing structure
2. Hotel brand image (actual or the way you wish it to be)
3. The fact that successful affiliate marketing is very time consuming

To make sound decisions how these will be affected by affiliate marketing, one has to understand the incentive structures of publishers and advertisers in affiliate marketing, because often, they can divert quite strongly.

The incentive structure for publishers in affiliate marketing
If a publisher places your ad on his website, he faces opportunity costs: He chooses your ad over someone else's on that particular spot on his webpage. Hence, he will search for the optimum advertisement, that is, the one for which he expects the highest return. In that case, his return equals commission from revenue generated by sales minus the acquisition cost he incurs from acquiring traffic. He will optimize his result by keeping acquisition

costs low and revenue high. For our purpose, we will look at revenue only, as it is the part with direct consequences for hotel marketing.

Revenue equals price times quantity, hence scoring high on both levers will bring up revenue. Quantity can be described as a function of price, the publisher must hence seek the optimum relation. Now, in affiliate marketing most publishers can only generate a relevant number of sales - and hence overall revenue - by offering high to very high discounts. The magic word here is "deals". Affiliate publishers are always hungry for discounted-price deals, it is what keeps their business going. As a basic rule, you can expect that publishers will require 20 or more percent off or require you to bring exclusive high-value goodies like, e.g. F&B vouchers, to the table in order for them to consider your listing. The logic behind is simple: Discounts simply sell, and affiliate publishers mostly cater to audiences that are extremely price sensitive and deal-thirsty.

Advertiser's incentives in affiliate marketing

Now let us consider the advertiser side, precisely, what incentives must prevail in order for affiliate marketing to be a useful addition to a hotel advertiser. We must recall a publisher's incentives in affiliate marketing: to publish deals. It follows that for advertisers, affiliate marketing becomes interesting in times of low demand when price cuts are a real option to reach desired levels of occupancy. In this case, incentives of publisher and advertiser are aligned, as both have an interested in reduced pricing to increase volume of bookings, or rooms sold. Consider the case in which you find it hard to bring your rooms to a satisfactory level of occupancy. You hit a certain plateau with your regular selling & pricing, above which you simply cannot get with your regular pricing structure. Fixed cost regression forces you to fill these rooms in order to reach your bottom line goal, so what to do? In such times of demand shortage, you have to push your product into the market. However, the predominant traffic generators of pull-marketing, SEO, SEM and Metasearch, are by definition not suitable to fill those times of need entirely.

Thus, stimulation of the demand side is needed. In other words, it is necessary to *create* attention, interest and desire among potential customers and then convert them into actual guests. Affiliates take over the task of customer acquisition, by directing traffic to the advertiser's website. When paid a commission, they also take over the risk of acquisition cost and hence, the conversion risk. Other modes of cooperation, such as CPC, CPM or fixed sum deals leave the risk of conversion with the advertiser.

Pitfalls to avoid – price and brand protection

As described above, although interests of publisher and affiliate are principally aligned in the case of deal promotion, affiliate marketing may in many cases pose a potential risk to hotel brand image, rooted in the way of traffic acquisition that most affiliate publishers rely on. The nature of deal marketing is highly competitive and publishers have to be extremely aggressive in acquiring traffic - they too, of course, rely on online marketing, which is costly. For obvious reasons, they are able to improve their cost-revenue-ratio by selling known and strong brands: Targeting users who are already who are actively looking will substantially increase the conversion rate of their offerings.

For publishers, using brand and hotel names in SEO and SEM presents itself as a viable way for acquiring traffic.

For you as a hotelier this means that you should explicitly forbid affiliates to use your brand/hotel name in online marketing. Traffic that is already actively looking for your brand is best absorbed directly by your website, without having to go through an affiliate - it is much more cost effective. To curb this possible negative side effect of affiliate marketing, follow these rules:

1. Define a set of keywords that you exclude from affiliate marketing, or prohibit SEM for your offers altogether

2. Do not provide deals to one particular affiliate too often, in order to limit his SEO-reach, and keep them from overly collecting content containing your brand. Competition on keywords is fierce and you do not want them to take your spot on the SERPs, as you want users to come directly to your website, without you having to pay commission to some publisher.

While curtailing affiliate marketing in SEM and SEO is one part of your brand protection formula, being picky about the brand image of your affiliate publisher is the other. For example, a very upscale brand in the 5-star luxury segment has decided to engage in affiliate marketing. When looking at publishers, various websites present themselves promising with impressive traffic numbers. However, looking at the domain names and brand logos of these publishers, many of them carry words like "deal", "clever", "cheap", "save" and the like. Obviously selling in a high price segment, the brand should carefully weigh pros and cons of affiliating its brand to such publisher names. Awareness for the risk of undermining the upscale brand image through affiliation with an everyday-low-prices-publisher is essential.

Investment and return: Affiliate marketing is time consuming

While affiliate networks take away some of the work that is necessary in acquiring and managing affiliate publishers, you will almost always have to contact publishers directly in order negotiate the details of your offer, if you want to be successful. Off-the-shelf offers pushed into a network will most likely not generate much response. It follows that you have to devote an expert whose job it will be to negotiate with publishers. Contacting and negotiating with publishers is time consuming, hence you should carefully calculate the return that affiliate marketing can achieve and compare it to investing the time and money in other channels.

Bottom line is, affiliate marketing can be very helpful in selling off "overcapacity" and positioning your website against OTAs in the deal-segment. The premise is that you can work the market right, generating website sales while safeguarding your price structure and brand.

Affiliate marketing and flash sales
The nature of affiliate marketing for hotels is very similar to the business model of flash dealers. Hence, affiliate marketing for the hotel website always runs in competition with flash sales. Being focused on offers of 30% and more below the regular market price, flash sales target the extremely price sensitive consumer segments. Demanding up to 30% of the gross rate, profitability of

such "deals" is chronically low. Although flash sales have their right to exist, they should be used only in balanced dosages. This is due to three reasons:

1. Flash deals can deteriorate the overall price level. With heavy use of flash deals, customers will get the impression of every-day-low-prices and over time, a hotel will not be able to enforce prices at the desired level.

2. Flash dealers often get their reach / visibility via affiliate partners. Once a flash deal is contracted, the hotel loses the control where it is displayed. A Hotel website's special deals will have to compete for affiliate attention, in case the hotel has a flash deal floating around at the time. This will of course increase the cost of sale with affiliates, as the abundance of offers will make those affiliates with reasonable reach demand marketing funds or higher CPOs from the hotel.

3. In order to squeeze out the maximum potential of a deal, most flash dealers are pretty lax on the standard for their affiliate marketing partners. Hence, a hotel might be selling on some dubious dumping website like inyourfacecheapprices.dealz.com where it should not appear. Diluting brand by working with deal-

websites is something that should be strictly avoided.

However, all three risks can be countered, eventually allowing for sound and effective affiliate marketing.

First on the list is the creation of black-lists of affiliate partners that can be considered a no-go and reach agreement with your flash sellers not to cooperate with the affiliates on that list. In doing so, the attractiveness of y hotel's own websites offerings and deals is leveraged, because highly price sensitive consumers learn over time that specials from the hotel do not come a-dime-a-dozen and that they are most likely to get the best prices on brand.com, plus it also avoids dilution of the brand image. The competition between a website's affiliate marketing and third party flash sales is not to be underestimated. Consequent monitoring of flash sale partner's activities is of the essence, if affiliate marketing is to be developed into a strategically relevant marketing channel.

Furthermore, exclusivity for a deal is never to be granted (if you can afford it). Whatever the offer of a flash seller is, it has to be sold on the hotel website, too. This makes sure that dependencies on a specific distribution partner are avoided. Actual and potential guests learn over time that the hotel website always has the best offer available.

An additional tip for single hotels: Affiliate marketing more than any other marketing channel relies on scalable publishing. That is, advertisers with just one hotel will have difficulties getting listed with relevant publishers, because placing their offering entails a very high risk - the product portfolio is simply too focused. For affiliate publishers, advertisers with large portfolios are preferable, because naturally, the probability for them to meet their price sensitive group's demands increases with the number of offerings. Unless the affiliate publisher concerned is super-focused[14], single hotel advertisers will be confronted with a relatively unattractive cost-benefit-ratio in affiliate marketing.

2.7. A Sledgehammer for Cracking Nuts: Display Marketing

Display marketing is the form of online marketing that most closely resembles traditional offline methods of marketing. It entails all forms of visual online marketing, that is, banner and video advertisements in all shapes and sizes. The function of display marketing, as opposed to other forms of online marketing, is not so much to generate direct sales but to capture views, and, to a lesser extent, clicks. It is comparatively ineffective in generating

---

[14] E.g., a website with content exclusively on baltic sea hotels.

direct bookings, and the following chapter will explain why this is the case.

To understand display advertising, it is first necessary to structure it along the possible modus operandi between advertiser and publisher. That is, the logic by which display ads are shown to internet users. The simplest way for an advertiser to place display advertising is to go into a bilateral agreement with a publisher, who will show the banner ad on his website. The commercial transaction between advertiser and publisher will usually be done in the form of a fixed media spent over time, as for example, having a banner advertising of a hotel on a particular webpage for 4 weeks. Such fixed sum media spending is not very risky for a publisher, as he is not concerned with the (short term) success of the advertisement, in the sense of views, clicks or even bookings. For the advertiser, choosing such a type of deal requires thorough knowledge of the type and quality of traffic that the publisher has; as he commits money ex ante, without the option of adjusting marketing spend along the way. To the advertiser the advantage of this type of online marketing is that costs do not scale with an increase on whatever KPI he is looking for – views, clicks, or bookings. E.g., spending 1.000 on the display ad may lead to 5.000 or 10.000 in revenue, depending on how well the advertisement performs. In theory, there is no limit to the return that can be generated from the ad, because costs do not increase with an increase in views, clicks or bookings.

However, this mechanism also works in the opposite direction. If the ad does not generate a sufficient amount of the desired responses, it will be highly inefficient, delivering returns of less than one or even zero. Unfortunately, experience shows that the latter case is the norm.

Another option in display marketing is the use of networks that allow for dynamically delivering advertisements to numerous publishers, who provide the advertiser with an audience suited to his product. For example, for a hotel such publishers are most likely found in the realm of travel and tourism. The network is a platform to which publishers and advertisers connect, which then allows placing advertisements on these websites at a per-thousand-impressions-price.[15] It collects all the requests for advertising space from numerous advertisers and matches it against its portfolio of publishers. The advantage here is that publisher compensation is per-thousand-ads delivered. This enables advertisers to scale reach far beyond just one or two websites. Such networks also provide the platform for a

---

[15] Examples of such a network would be the Google Display Network (GDN).

third, more sophisticated way of distributing online media: programmatic advertising. Here, the process of placing an ad on a website is enhanced by filigree algorithms that take into account various variables related to user behavior, such as browsing habits, correlating interests, demographics and the like, in order to decide in real time what ad to display. The algorithm over time becomes more and more precise, leading an improved quality of the audience, which in turn brings more high-quality traffic to the advertiser. Due to its dependency on large amounts of data for its algorithm, high media spend is necessary to provide a statistical valid amount of views and clicks. Programmatic is a very special case of online marketing, which I devoted a separate chapter to it later in the book.

The fourth and most effective form of display advertising is retargeting. The logic here is rather simple: Show an advertisement to a user who has already visited the website that is advertised. The retargeting mechanism delivers visuals to website visitors who are assumed to have not yet completed a transaction, but have been in contact with website and hence displayed a certain interest in the brand or hotel. The ad is to make the user recall the hotel and its offerings, come back to the website, and book. The reasoning behind is that visiting a website implies a user shows interest in that website's services, and by continuously exposing him to brand visuals, the user will eventually convert. From all display advertising, retargeting proves to be most effective when it comes to generating bookings.

Given these different varieties of display marketing, what place can this form of online marketing have in a hotel's online marketing strategy? The single most plausible reason for including this type of online marketing in to a strategy is its ability to indirectly leverage all other forms of online marketing. The way display marketing works is through repetition: attractive visuals, catchy videos and taglines continuously thrown at users will keep a hotel brand in their minds. However, such repetition is costly and of long duration, which is why display campaigns usually require large budgets. Combined with the fact they return very low conversion rates display campaigns are the least effective way of spending marketing funds.

Nonetheless, there are different forms of display advertising and they have varying degrees of effectiveness for direct bookings, which is why they should be analysed separately. The following order of priority stems from my personal experience on the effectiveness of the different types of display marketing. It can serve as guide for allocating funds if you *must* invest in display marketing.

1. *Retargeting* – Always keep a retargeting campaign running for your hotel. Targeting users who have already shown some interest in your hotel is most likely to deliver direct bookings, plus it enhances brand awareness. Although conversion rates are much lower than in SEM or Metasearch, they are typically among the highest of display marketing formats. Conversion rates above 0.5% are reasonable, but if campaigns and visuals are managed right, conversion rates can go up as high as 1%.

2. *Bilateral agreements* – Keep these sporadic and do your research on the publisher you want to cooperate with. Does he have an audience that suits your product? For example, five star luxury travel or design aficionados looking for trips to Europe's hottest destinations? Is his traffic volume significant? Do you have an interesting offer in place? Then you might want to consider placing your visual on his website. In this regard, see also the chapter on affiliate marketing – the essence of cooperation is the same as in bilateral display partnerships.

3. *Programmatic advertising* – Programmatic advertising may make sense in times where the goal is to create mass attention, without coupling a direct sales target to it. For example, in the ramp up phase of new hotels. Due to its high reach and improved targeting, programmatic *can* be effective for simply "getting the message out". Aside from being extremely costly, this form of advertising has severe downsides, in particular for stand-alone hotels not being part of a bigger chain. In fact, the pitfalls with this type of marketing are so grave that they are examined in a separate chapter later on in this book.

4. *Simple Display Advertising on Networks* – Not as effective as retargeting and programmatic, display advertising without algorithmic optimization, "simple" display advertising on display networks can pay in brand awareness. However, do not expect direct bookings from this type of display marketing. The effectiveness of simple display advertising is so low, because it lacks any form of audience targeting, that the other forms of display marketing have.[16] Hence, I suggest

considering this form of marketing only once all other marketing channels are maxed out.

A concluding note on the monitoring necessary to manage display marketing: Be extra careful when you engage in display marketing, especially programmatic advertising. The scattering effects in this type of marketing are very high for advertisers that have a very narrow and limited product portfolio, such as a single hotel or small hotel chain. For these, large marketing budgets are necessary in order to actually feed targeting algorithms to a degree where they can make sense of the observed data. And even in case the algorithms have detected a target group that returns adequate click rates, the limited product portfolio will return conversion rates that return ROAS far from attractive. This is why in any form of display marketing, you should have a close watch on performance - daily KPI monitoring is of the essence, in order to identify overly wasteful campaigns and stop them. This problem receives leverage through the fact that a lot of traffic on websites is comprised by bots. Bots are not human users, but machines running over website to identify certain aspects of it, such as text and pictures,

---

[16] Recall the types of targeting: retargeting caters to website visitors, programmatic to algorithmically defined audiences and bilateral agreements target via the human element that decides on what publisher to work with.

or to perform defined tasks, such as clicking on a link. Consequently you pay for impressions (or views) that are without value.

2.8. Creative Works: Content Marketing

"Content is king" - this slogan is still a buzz phrase in online marketing. Unfortunately, few practitioners have ever been able to exactly denote what this actually means. What is content, what is high quality, and how does it affect sales? In the following chapter, I will break down the issue into two areas: the *creation of content* and its *application in marketing*. It is necessary to differentiate between the two in order to fully understand the role of content in online marketing, and in particular, what it can do for hotels.

The term "content" generally refers to any type of text or visual (video, picture) that is placed on a website. It serves an informational purpose for users, as it describes or represents a product or service, which is to be sold on a website. From a marketing point of view, the idea of "quality content", however, goes beyond the mere informational purpose. Content is not just descriptive information, such as, "these are our hotel rooms and wireless LAN, minibar and amenities are included". Quality content distinguishes itself from pure description content in that it fulfills a special interest or need of users in and of itself. It creates emotions and emotional attachment by going beyond a simple service presentation. One could say, quality content "tells a story". Examples of such attachment of quality content on hotel websites are emotions like fun, belonging or relaxation, i.e. emotions that arise when a user engages with content. For instance, by presenting its exotic and lively culture, a web page may bring about interest in a destination. For obvious reasons, visual content like pictures and videos are more useful for creating such emotional response. Whether it is the surroundings of a hotel, the local city, the hotel itself or its outlets, picture video content that brings users to feel excitement is "high quality".

Quality content engages users by giving them something they enjoy for its own sake (like watching a fun video) and at the same time subtly promoting your services (i.e. hotel). Put into the right context, quality content is able increase your brand awareness among potential customers and positively affects the conversion performance of all your online marketing channels.

However, the challenge in producing quality hotel content is scalability. After a certain time, new content has to be created, which is of course costly. Hence, the decision to invest in high quality content should take into consideration the life-cycle of the content and the possible return it is able to generate. The problem here is, however, that measuring life-cycle and return on investment in content is quite difficult. Naturally, one can test, for example, running a video against a picture on a hotel landing page and check whether this results in an increase in clicks or conversions (whatever you are testing for). Then, monitoring views, clicks and bounce rates over time will indicate whether the content is still effective, or whether it has worn off.

However, measuring the effectiveness of content in relation to direct bookings is not that clear. Quality content entails branding effects that may translate into bookings over a longer period of time, with high delay between the time of content interaction and the time of booking. Correlating or even causally linking content with increases in bookings requires one to filter out the "noise" that does as well impact direct bookings, which is time consuming and requires a high level of analytical skill.

For example, you may run multiple tests on your website for design, functionalities, taglines, etc. simultaneously. Although each component is measurable separately at a time, synergetic effects are not accurately measured, because it is either too costly or time consuming. The same problem applies to quality content and changes in content. A good way of overcoming the limitations of this approach is to use website content on social media. Because on social media tracking ability of interaction with content is most precise and extensive, and responses can be measured immediately, it allows testing for non-financial proxies, which allow for judging the success of content. Such proxies are followers, tweets, shares, and clicks to website from the respective social media channel. Observing these will indicate whether the respective content creates the type of desired interaction that eventually feeds into brand image and brand awareness. E.g., a high number of positive comments or a high number of shares and likes indicates that users have a favorable attitude to a particular piece of content. Hence, it may make sense to create a line of content from that particular piece, invest more into its production, and putting it on your website.

Creating such content basically involves some form of storytelling. You want to create a story that is interesting enough to catch on to users, but that still allows you to hint at your hotel and its amenities. By having the user engage with your content, you want to give him that little nudge to book on your website, as the content generated interest and desire for your hotel/brand. The challenge here is that the hotel industry is a largely commoditized business, in which stories that are interesting and deliver direct bookings are hard to come by, although the hospitality and travel industry is, theoretically, the perfect ground for interesting stories to be told. While is true to some extent, a fundamental characteristic of the hotel industry limits hotels in the amount of engaging content they can produce.

That travel and tourism provides a perfect ground for storytelling is true for websites that provide large scale travel advice to extremely big audiences.[17] Covering any thinkable destination in the world, information on everything from sights to restaurants to hotels, and even having a substantial user base that generates part of the content, of course allows for the production of quality content, or stories for that matter, *on a regular basis*.

The average hotel however cannot dispose of such resources. Imagine a small chain of 10 hotels, located in 7-8 different cities in Central Europe. How many stories can it really create? Most likely, it will run into creative trough after 10-20 quality content pieces, or stories. To produce more content, which inevitably will be detached from the hotel's own character, but will have to focus on surrounding events and locations, the hotel group will have to invest heavily in creative resources, either by hiring a content marketer for creative ideas, or by employing an agency.

In addition to the money spent on personnel or agencies, it will also have to invest in the writing of copy

---

[17] For example, websites like Tripadvisor or Yelp.

(moderately expensive, if done well), production of pictures (very expensive if done professionally), and videos (for most hotels, out-of-their-league-expensive). On top of that there will be website development costs: quality content pieces should have an individual section on the website, such as a blog, which may demand individual programming or buying a SaaS solution. This is why I advise to thoroughly calculate the cost and possible return of content marketing, even if relying on proxies for determination of returns. Be aware that in contrast to money spent in performance marketing, the payoff of content marketing is not very predictable, so in particular for the tight budgeted hotelier, spending money on content marketing can result in a low-return endeavor.

A final recommendation on the production of content: When designing content, stick to competencies and knowledge that you have inhouse. For example, you have inhouse expertise on wellness and SPA treatments, or you have a fantastic restaurant. In that case you can create interesting stories around beauty care and grooming, or cooking and wine tasting, respectively. Other themes that offer themselves for the creation of interesting stories are golf, tennis, watersports and the like (if you are in that kind of resort business), broad scale events to a certain degree (at least some content possibilities for business hotels), if happening regularly. Also, depending on your location and target customer segment, music and arts might provide some ground for content creation.

In any case, do not try to write about stuff you have no in-depth knowledge about. E.g., if you do not have an insider in your team with the inside-scoop on the hottest spots in your destination's nightlife, do not attempt to write about it. The problem here is that you cannot judge whether the content produced is sensible and provides utility and information to your users. More often than not, it will go under in the endless amount of exchangeable happy talk on the web.

The Quick Win: Local Information Services

The term "local information services" denotes the structured data that is available on websites, such as search engines or social media platforms, to provide users with the contact data of businesses, such as restaurants, shops, or in our case, hotels. The data available includes telephone numbers, address, email, website / domain, basic pictures and customer reviews.

Local information services[18] have gained increased relevance because of the expanding dominance of mobile device usage, especially because of users looking up information on businesses and their local surroundings on their mobile devices. The list of local information services existing is extensive, with differing regional or local relevance.[19]

Although it seems trivial, the simple act of keeping information on local information services up-to-date is an easy lever for increased direct bookings. Information includes contacts details like telephone number or email, but also pictures of rooms, outlets and amenities. There is no specific knowledge necessary here, only a few hands

---
[18] Examples of which are search engines, map services, social media and review websites.
[19] For example, the dominant local information service in the US may play no role in France, and vice versa.

with the time to manage such accounts. The effect is not be underestimated, as many users have such a service as their first or second online touch point when looking for hotels. Having contact details, website domain and polished pictures on your local profile helps to create the immediate contact between hotel and guest, without middleman - such as OTAs involved. User frustration because of lacking or wrong direct contact information results in users turning to OTAs, even when they already made the decision to book a particular hotel. Local profiles are particularly relevant if outlets such as a spa or restaurant carrying an individual name and/or own brand identity exist in a hotel and the outlet relies on a local audience in addition to hotel guests.

3. All Tinsel and Glitter - A Critical View on Current Hypes

Chapter 2 presented the relevant online marketing channels and carved out their pros and cons. In order to provide a full view of online marketing, I thought it necessary to include an extra excursus on a few topics that are particularly loaded with hype. They are more or less contemporary phenomena that promise(d) to be "the next big thing" in online marketing. As it is possible to quickly waste a lot of money on these marketing measures without seeing returns, a closer look at them is necessary. To preclude, they should not receive active consideration in your marketing strategy, unless you have an appetite for risk and some budget to toy around with.

3.1. Influencer Marketing

A very recent development in the hemisphere of social media is influencer marketing. Influencer marketing in principle refers to someone paying somebody else to write a story about his product or service. Things get interesting when that someone has a huge online following and when this following is actually interested in what this person does, states, or shares. When such a following interacts with the person (via blogs or social media) and is receptive for his or her opinion, then this following is potentially being *influenced* by that person – this is what the term *influencer* means. From a business point of view, this means that such an influencer may convince others to make certain purchasing decisions.

It is a legitimate approach to think of this in terms of return-on-investment, as such accumulated purchasing decisions of followers can make it worthwhile to pay the influencer a certain amount of money in order to promote or directly sell one's products or services.

Supercharged with stories of success from influencers, loaded with high-class picture and video material and thousands or millions of likes and followers, influencer marketing has become all the hype in many industries. However, for the largest part of the hotel industry, influencer marketing does not work, at least not if you are looking for a reasonable return and do take into account its opportunity cost.

Most business success stories about influencer marketing take place in the realm of fast moving consumer goods, especially clothes and cosmetics. These are by their very nature products with a very high potential for endorsement: Comparatively low financial investment in the product and the potential for impulse buying are product features that elegantly fit to the short term, one-off impact of influencer posts. However, for hotels the story is different. Reason being that we are confronted with the same challenge of scalability that applies to social media and content marketing, with the addition of three further, very important limitations:

> By nature, particularly the *young audiences with low to very low purchasing power* are those that are receptive to be influenced in their purchasing decisions by "influencer marketing". Thus, unless you cater exclusively to young audiences, you are confronted with low probabilities for generating bookings from influencer posts.

> An influencer is only as interesting as his last post. The *short term nature* of social media peaks out in influencer marketing. Once the next post appears in an influencer's timeline or blog, sales potential of your piece decreases sharply. With the second, third and fourth post following, it approaches zero. As you have little control over the behavior of the influencer and what he posts next, your window of opportunity (in terms of time) thus tends be extremely small.

> A *high number of frauds* are active in this field. Given its hype and newness, influencer marketing by its very nature tends to attract frauds and me-too-individuals. It sounds like a venturer's dream: A lot of money for almost no work, and with hotels, you even get to travel! The consequence of such bright promise is that many bandwagon-influencers exist, of which some simply buy their following by acquiring a follower base of fake profiles, have a self-referential following or simply lack any relevant following at all.

The combination of these factors indicates that influencer marketing can be a risky endeavor. On any dimension measured, from clicks to ROAS, other means of online marketing outperform influencer marketing by far.

I admit, the three arguments above are somewhat polemic, and do not convince the more scientifically minded hotelier. One may argue rightly that the three arguments do not speak against influencer marketing generally, but simply mandate that one should be careful and look with scrutiny at the influencers one chooses to work with. The argument is fair, so let us assume for the moment a case in which all three factors are averted and the respective influencer actually has an organic and engaged following, posts with reasonable frequency and has an audience with decent purchasing power. Still, I will argue that the *budget risk* of engagement for the hotelier remains high, for the following reasons:

1. **Attention of audiences concentrates on a short tail of content.** If you look at influencer audiences as a collective construct, their attention concentrates among very few pieces of content. The very long tail of small scale and mediocre influencers produces content that is, by online marketing standards, almost irrelevant. The sizes of subsets of this audience with interest in content pieces along the longtail decrease the further down the long tail you go, as illustrated by Figure 2. It follows that the more focused your product is (hotels are by their very nature very focused products - think location), the farther down the long tail the influencers' content piece will be. Hence limited visibility and very little interaction on the content.

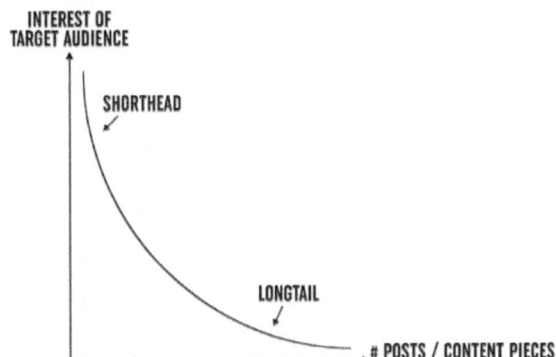

Figure 2 - Shorthead and Longtail in Audience Attention

2. **Attention spans of audiences.** However, managing to be in the short tail is not a guarantee for success in itself. Influencer content has no longevity, because of the incredible frequency with which content is produced and published. Competition for audience attention is fierce online and the half-life of content is small. This means, if the influencer post is not able to immediately (i.e. within a day or two) generate attention, the money spent to produce it has gone to waste. Cases in which original content is dug up at a later time and only then starts to attract attention are practically non-existent.

3. **Few control and steering mechanisms available.** Generally, influencers demand that

they can determine the type and quality of the content they produce without ex-ante interference or specifications from sponsors. Engaging with an influencer on the term that content is produced at his or her sole discretion, means that little to no measures to correct it exist. E.g., if the picture or video material he or she produced is crappy, it will be discovered *after the fact*, i.e. when the stay at the hotel is over. Continuation of the cooperation with the influencer is unlikely; however, costs for the initial piece of work are sunk. Furthermore, there are no means to inquire on the actual quality, that is, the match between the influencer's follower base and your hotel's desired target group, beforehand. Follower numbers and interaction KPIs (i.e. clicks) tell you little about whether the follower base is actually relevant to your particular offer or hotel. Unless of course the influencer is super-niche and you are looking for someone just like that, e.g., an influencer focusing on hiking in the Austrian Alps. However, such a niche influencer is unlikely to have a sizeable following.

Do not be fooled by the craze surrounding influencer marketing - it is simply not designed to have sustainable sales effects. Hence, when it comes to allocating advertisement funds, I strongly suggest staying away from it. Only when sufficient play money is at hand that cannot be spend effectively in other channels, a shot at influencer marketing is justified. Under no circumstance one should work with influencers because of fear of missing out, or because some marketing agency is hyping it as the next big thing.

3.2. Programmatic Advertising

Programmatic advertising, due to its algorithmic nature and comparatively complex mechanisms of advertisement distribution, is considered the holy grail of display marketing. The argument, why programmatic advertising is the superior form of display marketing (and sometimes marketing in general), primarily rests on the targeting options that it offers:

By employing a sophisticated algorithm, a provider of a programmatic display advertising network learns *over time* what advertisement-publisher combinations work best for a given goal (clicks or conversions), which is specified by the advertiser. The algorithm then continues to learn what combinations work best in regard to the goal. Collecting more and more of these data points, the algorithm is ultimately able to determine the optimum advertisement, delivered at the optimal time on a specific publisher page. Thus, this form of advertising is extremely efficient at generating return for the advertiser, because it allows reducing or even eliminating the typical inefficiencies that are connected to display marketing. Consequently, a programmatic platform will have exclusive access to a network of high value travel data and publishers, which allows them a very precise targeting of users. For instance, showing a hotel ad to someone who has booked a flight for the respective destination on another website.[20]

So much for the theory. The problem with this theory is that it does not transfer to practice for most hotels, in particular small hotel groups or single hotels. Programmatic advertising is heavily reliant on extremely high volumes of data that must be fed to algorithms in order for them to extract any sensible information from the click behavior of users, and consequently optimize the underlying display campaign. From this precondition follows a requirement for mobilizing massive budgets for even the smallest campaigns. Running a programmatic campaign for 4-6 weeks for a single hotel easily requires a five digit (Dollar- or Euro-) budget. The average value of your hotel bookings must be accordingly high in order to produce even a moderate return on this kind of ad spend.

For instance, say you start with the absolute minimum of 10,000 EUR for your campaign, and the average booking value is 200 EUR, then in order to produce a moderate return of 5 (which is the equivalent to a 20% COS) you will need to generate revenue of 50,000 EUR, or 250 bookings. By all standards, the probability for this to

---

[20] This is why some refer to this as "pre-targeting", which is, targeting groups/audiences that seem likely to book on your website because some of their traits resemble those of a target group that has actually shown interest in your hotel.

happen is rather low. Display is among the worst performing marketing measure in terms of conversion rates (less than 0.4% is common) and even the sophisticated algorithms ca do little to change that. Quite the opposite in fact, the mathematical necessity for high volumes of click data inevitably creates high inefficiencies at the start of the campaign, because media is "just thrown out there" and only over time ineffective media formats, publisher websites, display times and the combinations thereof are weeded out.

Thus, as programmatic advertising relies on algorithms to continuously improve performance (the right visual at the right time for the right audience), it is extremely inefficient at the start of a campaign and only gradually becomes more efficient over time. This means that for the algorithm to "learn", it needs high loads of input data to separate low performing rules from high performing rules, which means that a lot of impressions are wasted in the initial phase of a programmatic advertising campaign. Given this circumstance, it follows that this type of advertising is more suitable for chains and larger groups, which are able to integrate high numbers of hotels or special offerings across hotels into one single campaign. For single hotels the story is different. Naturally, the potential target group for a single hotel is much narrower defined than the target group for an entire group of hotels. This means that for a stand-alone hotel, a display visual will initially be shown to a high number of users that are completely out of the relevant target group. Reason being that the algorithm has little information on where to start, i.e. it does not know where displaying the advertisement works best, as the data points for starting a campaign are few in number. Larger groups are able to compensate for this effect by having more starting points and also in creating spillover effects from traffic that might not fit the actual advertisement. E.g. someone being shown an ad for a hotel in Berlin might not be interested in Berlin, but end up on a page for the group's hotel in Hamburg, a destination the user is actually interested in. This information is then used by the algorithm to determine performance rules based on statistical validity, in order to determine the optimum advertisement delivery. However, even for larger hotel groups programmatic still requires to move large budgets into this form of advertising, while producing comparatively low returns. Hence, ad spend is better allocated in other marketing channels and only once their potential is fully exploited, programmatic can be added to the online marketing mix.

3.3. Fixed Fee Affiliate Marketing: The Media Partner Model

A comparatively young phenomenon has been the approach of some publisher deal-websites to not operate on the basis of a commission/CPO, cost-per-view, or cost-per-click, but to require a one-time fixed fee payment for a blog post, social media post, newsletter position or a combination thereof. This very basic form of affiliate marketing can be described as a "media deal", where the advertiser simply buys advertising space for a fixed fee, without any performance commitment on the side of the publisher. Hence the term "media partner".

The nature of this publisher model is to present only heavily discounted deals, similar to a flash seller, that are published to a very price sensitive follower base that is highly motivated to finding very low priced travel deals. In an attempt to capitalize on this potential, the publisher then turns to hotels, OTAs, airlines and the like, offering them to buy advertising space in the form of posts that link to the respective offerings on the advertisers' websites. As this fee model is usually up-front and fixed-sum, the entire conversion risk is carried by the advertiser. This distribution of conversion risk is in itself not problematic; however, it bears a high probability of wasting money when analyzed according to the traffic quality that such publishers provide. First, their targeting is rather unspecific: Although the total follower base might be high, the relevant target group with at least mild interest for the advertiser's specific offering can be - and usually is - very small. Second, the targeting of highly price sensitive customers creates potential for brand dilution. Because price sensitive customers lust for dumping prices and "deals", media partner publishers will only publish highly discounted rates, which is of course, diametrically opposed to an advertiser's principal interest to enforce high prices. Accordingly, high absolute returns are only achieved if the absolute number of bookings generated is also high. Recall that revenue is price times quantity - the price of such deals has to be 50 or more percent off the average rate, which has to be compensated by the number of bookings generated to reach a revenue level with a gross margin greater than zero. E.g. deals of this type usually are offered in ranges between 500 and 5,000 (Euro/Dollar) per offer.

In this type of publishing deal, incentives of advertiser and publisher are not aligned. The problem becomes evident when looking at the concept of fixed fee publishing deals: If a publisher knows, he will deliver a respectable number of sales, why should he put all the marketing investment risk on the advertiser? If he takes a commission, he participates with every sale he makes. If he takes a fixed sum, he does not, but has a safe income, regardless of how the published offer performs. Such media deals are not really incentive compatible on the part of the publisher. Incentive compatibility is one of the main concepts one has to understand in order to manage the publisher-advertiser-relationship. This is why I advise to stay away from non-performance based "media deals" and stick to performance based marketing measures that compensate the publisher on a per-click or per-booking basis. Deals where the publisher entails no click or conversion risk are not aligned to advertiser's incentives and hence should have no place in any performance based online marketing strategy.

3.4. Big Data and Data Driven Marketing

The terms "big data" and "data driven marketing" have been all the hype over the last 2-3 years. Although the hype is wearing off at the time of writing this, the terms have found their way into online marketing terminology. As there are numerous services and products marketed in the name of the above terms, I felt it necessary to break down what they actually mean, in order to keep readers from tumbling into investments in services and software they actually have no need for.

First, there is need for clarification what big data means for hotels, in particular what it can do for small hotel chains and single hotels. In the context of online marketing, big data refers to the process of collecting large amounts of information on guests and users, and making use of that data to continuously refine marketing and communication campaigns, ultimately in an effort to sell more. For both data collection and data analysis to happen, you need software. For this need, smart companies have developed software products to address it. The selling proposition of these products can be summed up as follows: Collect additional data and more of it with our software, and then our software will analyze that data in order to allow for improved campaign results.

The following paragraphs will sketch out what this actually means for online marketing for hotels and why the average hotelier should not overestimate what big data can do, despite it being attributed revolutionary and game-changing possibilities by its proponents.

The case for data driven marketing can be broken down into three arguments: a) You need more data, which b) you have to analyze in a more sophisticated way to c) apply the insights from analysis to bring your online marketing to the next level. The case seems logical: analyze more data, bring deeper insights about your users/guests into your marketing tactics and improve revenue results of campaigns. However, structuring the essence of the argument will show that this is not a law and that more data does not automatically mean better results.

First, one has to define what the word data means. Data is a nice word, because it allows to suggest numerous positive qualities in the term it describes, and to the person or entity using it. Using the word data in conjunction with managerial lingo like marketing, online marketing or management suggests that what is being referred to is very scientific, informative, accurate and generally brings about better results than its non-data counterparts. It lends itself easily to load up meaning onto otherwise trivial and tautological facts. However, basically everything you do in management is somehow data driven. Even if you only make decisions based on assumptions about reality, you rely on some type of data, since these assumptions have to feed off from some information about reality – i.e. "data". Hence, the word data can be any sort of information about reality, for example, the reality of user direct booking behavior. In the context of online marketing, data driven usually denotes some form of advanced tracking of user's online behavior with which supposedly better ad spending decisions are achieved.

The question now is whether more data is also always better, because this is what data driven implies. If you act "data driven", you rely on large quantities of data to reach decisions and the more data you have, the better your decisions will be. However, it seems justified to pose the question what is to be gained from this. Collecting data just for the sake of having more data does not add any value to the quality of your decisions.

To answer the question fully, one has to refer to two general characteristics of data:

1. Data has *decreasing marginal utility* attached to it. For all decisions, there exists a point where additional data collected does not provide any additional knowledge. No new insight is gained from the

additional data, although technically, the amount of knowledge increases. One might simply learn more facts, but it is not possible to derive any meaningful actions from the knowledge of these facts. As a rule of thumb, the 80/20-rule applies to the field of online marketing and data: With 20% of the data, 80% of the insights on how to steer online marketing are gathered.

2. Collecting more data demands more knowledge on *how to analyze and interpret* that data on the side of the collector. That is, you will always require a human component that is able to make sense of all the data your "machine" gathered. If the analytical talent is not available to extract the value out of data, it is itself useless.

Now, this is not to make a case against data collection and working on the basis of numbers and facts, instead of gut feeling, opinions and impressions. Quite the opposite in fact: It is absolutely necessary to manage online marketing on the basis of quantitative data. But in the very act of working with (quantitative) data you will find that there are limits to the insights gained from data collection. The above points should illustrate that more data is not always better and that the cost of data collection must be carefully weighed against its benefits.

Hence, before acquiring expensive services for data collection, be sure that what the service can do for you actually adds value to your marketing that justifies the cost.

4. Managing for Success - How to Get the Most out of Ad Spend

The previous chapter has presented the toolset a hotelier has available. The following chapter will show how to use this toolset most effectively by carving out a unique and truly performance based approach to managing all online marketing channels in concerted action. Factors from areas adjoining online marketing and guidelines on how to treat them are presented. You will learn what factors are of high priority and how to translate the insights you gained in the previous chapter into action: How a strategy should be set up, what measures are most important and how to apply them. Also, you will learn why your online marketing strategy should be integrated in your overall distribution strategy, and why the best results in online marketing are achieved through concerted actions in the overall distribution management.

4.1. Limitations of Marketing Budget Allocation

A fundamental necessity to gain momentum on website bookings is the perspective taken on the costs of producing website bookings. A widespread phenomenon in the hospitality industry is the wish to increase the share of direct bookings paired with an unwillingness to invest in the means necessary to acquire those bookings. This inconsistency between demand and action is due to a flawed but still predominant understanding the industry has of how direct bookings are generated, and the perspective taken on the cost of online marketing.

The flawed understanding relates to the idea that website/direct bookings are free of cost. The flaw lies in the assumption that by simply having a website online direct bookings come in at virtually zero cost: Once the investment in programming the website is depreciated, direct bookings are free of charge. The problem with this perspective is that it completely disregards the fact website traffic is never free, except for the one case where a user enters a domain directly in the address bar of his browser. This type of traffic will represent only a fraction of overall website traffic, the remainder must be purchased via the types of publishers described in this book. The costs of such "purchasing" is whatever has to paid for clicks and views in the respective online marketing channels. The problem in understand the nature of these costs lies in the term online marketing, which associates ad spend with actual "marketing" costs. The term marketing, however, for many managers and hoteliers is (unknowingly) connected to the idea of diffuse spending on displays, billboards, catalogues, brochures and the like. These items (usually) do not allow for calculating a return. Hence, they are viewed upon strictly from a cost perspective, in the sense that they cost money but do not directly generate revenue. Pure cost items are first on the list for cost cutting, or, at least, tend to be the items under constant scrutiny. Because of a lack of differentiation, this includes online marketing.

When it comes to OTA commissions, hotels have a different view. Commissions are complained about being too high or increasing, however, they are considered part of distribution costs, which themselves are accepted as a given for bringing in revenue. It is easy to understand the relation between commission and revenue, as the former is a percentage of the latter. It follows that when observing an increase in commission cost, the implication must be that revenue has also increased. This is why practical limits on absolute commission payments dot not exist - the hotelier understands that revenue has increased too, which is why he will not cut off distribution of the respective commission-based distribution partners. For example, even if budgeted commissions on the 15th of the month are exceeded, the OTA will not be cut off from production.

Knowing about the nature of online bookings and the competition for visibility online, as depicted in the earlier chapters of this book, it is necessary to set aside this outdated perspective on spend on online marketing. Although online marketing is often put into the same category as offline marketing with levity, its nature is entirely different: Because of tracking technology, spend in online channels are (usually) directly attributable to generated revenue and vice versa. Denoting online marketing spend as the COS of direct booking revenue, it becomes directly comparable to OTA commissions, which allows for a more appropriate perspective: online marketing (i.e. ad spend) is a form of distribution cost: Ad spend represents the commission necessary to generate direct bookings. For the hotelier interested in increasing online direct revenue, applying the traditional view on marketing budget to *online* marketing funds brings about severe limitations on the potential absolute and relative direct revenue increase that can be accomplished. That is why I suggest viewing online marketing spend as a form of distribution cost in order to max out the potential of your online marketing campaigns. To understand why and how this simple change of perspective opens upon opportunities, it is necessary to understand the logic and relationship between online revenue and cost.

Generally, the relation between online revenue and online marketing funds allows to express any ad spend as a cost-per-booking by dividing the marketing spend of a specified campaign by the revenue that is attributed to that campaign. The resulting ratio tells at what price direct booking revenue is "bought" on the hotel website. The number allows comparing the efficiency of selling via the hotel website to other channels, for example OTAs. For instance, a booking on an OTA might cost 10% on the dollar, whereas the cost of online marketing for direct booking revenue adds up to 8% on the dollar.

What happens when online marketing is managed on a pure cost-and-budget-perspective? Of course, allocated funds will be used until they are depleted. In proceeding that way, a ceiling for direct booking revenue is set. For example, a online marketing manager working exclusively on a set budget will stop his ongoing marketing activities in the middle of the month because he ran out of funds. All marketing channels are scaled down to zero ad spend. However, if ad spend is zero because funds are depleted, traffic on the website dries up and bookings will scale down accordingly. This means the hotel will have to rely on third parties to bring in business for the rest of the month. The game starts over at the first of the next month when fresh money is available to the manager. In this way of management, money is left at the table, which OTAs are more than happy to grab.

Thus, I suggest that the question of how much to invest on ad spend is approached best from the perspective of ROAS/COS perspective, instead of using cost budgeting. The underlying argument for this approach is provided by the law of transparency in online competition: Any online sales channel is at every point in time in direct competition with all other accessible online sales channels. That is, a hotel website is not a sales channel operating in a closed hemisphere, but is always in direct competition with OTAs, tour operators and all other channels that distribute a hotel's rooms online. At a mouse click, users have all rates and availabilities ready, prices are at any point in time comparable. It is of the essence to understand that virtually *all* of these channels rely on the same means of traffic acquisition. Hence, they are competing for traffic, and an additional visitor for one website might be a lost visitor to another. It follows that every lever available has to be pulled to direct traffic to a hotel's website, away from competition like OTAs. Cost budgeting ad spend is not very well suited to achieve the maximization of traffic acquisition, as outlined above.

Instead, the maximization of traffic, and hence direct booking revenue, requires a management mechanism that sets the actual return on ad spend in focus. This approach I term Cost-of-Sale-Management - it is the key driver in extracting the most utility from online marketing campaigns for hotels.

4.2. Cost-of-Sale Management

The first step towards understanding online marketing as a form of distribution cost is to familiarize with concept of *attribution modelling*. All online marketing channels have spillover effects, in particular display advertising and social media may bring visibility to a hotel that does not translate into immediate direct bookings. However, they present a first touch point between hotel website and user/guest, influencing the user along his booking journey. The user may ultimately book on the hotel website by entering the domain name in his browser or by clicking on a search ad, in a later point in time on his user journey. This circumstance allows for attributing a certain share of the revenue that was generated through the booking to the display ad or the social media post that started the user journey. Attribution modelling is the act of trying to determine exactly what the value of the share should be. It describes the act of attributing overall website revenue to overall online marketing spending, with each marketing dollar spent on a certain channel being expressed as a percentage of your revenue. The idea behind this modelling is to quantify what the spillover between channels actually translates into in terms of revenue. Knowing the exact share of contribution to revenue then allows to precisely allocate budgets across online marketing channels for optimum revenue growth.

The following example describes how attribution modelling works in practice:

Say our average booking value is 100 Euro in revenues and we want to know what each online marketing channel contributes to these 100 Euros. Using according attribution software, we track the customer journey and all views and clicks that resulted in some form of contact between users and our hotel website. As we are not concerned with delving into the technology behind this type of tracking, we only look at the result presented to us. The software returns the information that, on average, the channel contribution to revenue of our online marketing looks as follows:

60% SEM - The last click before booking that brought users to the website.
20% Display - The booker had been shown a retargeting visual of the hotel on some other website before he conducted the above search.
20% Social Media advertising - The initial point of contact in the journey; Bookers had been shown an ad on social media, clicked on it and landed on our website

The percentage values denote the share of tracked revenue via a channel in relation to the amount of users that came into contact with the channel (measured in ad views or clicks). Now, the conclusion regarding the allocation of funds is that one unit of additional funds for SEM will raise revenue by 60%, retargeting by 20% and social media also by 20%. If tracking is accurate, we can now steer online marketing without having to worry about budgets in these channels, as we can expect a given return when allocating additional funds. This is the first step towards understanding online marketing as a form of distribution cost. However, there are two downsides to attribution modelling in this form. First, it requires using tracking software that is integrated with all your online marketing channels - this costs money. Second, the notion of budget is still used for managing the channels, which impedes the comparability of the cost of website bookings against OTA and other third party bookings.

To overcome both limitations, a management approach based on a percentage value for overall website revenue (i.e. direct booking revenue) is necessary. This is what I call Cost-of-Sale Management, or COS Management.

This approach to steering online marketing views the website as one singular distribution channel that is fed by the entirety of all online marketing activities. It follows that for this distribution channel its level of cost can be represented as a percentage value, in dividing revenue by the sum of all online marketing spend. The result is the COS-value.

Cost-of-Sale for Website Bookings

$$\text{COS Website} = \frac{\text{Sum of all Online Marketing Costs}}{\text{Total Website Revenue}}$$

The COS-value hence denotes the overall ad spend necessary to generate one unit of direct booking revenue. In the remainder of chapter, we will look at how this concept can be applied to managing the allocation of "budget" to marketing channels in order to achieve optimum revenue growth.

In order to develop a practical approach to online marketing management for growth, it is essential to understand the law of decreasing marginal utility and why it describes a very real law in online marketing. The law of decreasing marginal utility in its basic form says with increasing numbers of a good, the utility from an additional unit of a good, or more generally a "thing", is decreasing. For example, money is a good with decreasing marginal utility: If I have a total wealth of ten Dollars, the utility received from an additional Dollar is comparatively high, probably as high as the value of each of the previous ten Dollars to me. However, if my total wealth amounts to one million Dollars, the value of an additional Dollar is less than for the first one million Dollars.

In the realm of online marketing spend, this logic applies to the return generated by additional marketing funds: The first thousand spent on SEM may return ten thousand in revenue, hence an ROAS of 10:1, or inversely viewed a COS of 10%. Now, the next thousand spent in SEM may only return 8,000 in revenue, i.e. a ROAS of 8:1, or a COS of 12.5%. Hence, the relation between funds spent on SEM and revenue is not linear, but the return from spending additional monetary units decreases. In other words, the marginal return on ad spend (ROAS) is decreasing. It implies that even with an unlimited budget for online marketing, there is an absolute limit to the amount of revenue that can be produced in using this budget.

Consequently, this also means that for any given COS-value, there exists a maximum number of bookings that can be produced. For example, say the first 100 bookings on our website come in at a COS of 10%, but booking number 101 does cost more at the margin, the COS for this booking may be 10.5%.

Figure 3 shows this relation as a COS-curve, where there exists an ultimate cut-off point x, where the delta in revenue is zero and additional ad spend does not return more utility: the ROAS equals zero.

The curve allows to be translated into a simple equation: Find your maximum COS along the curve in order to achieve cost-optimized revenue growth. When first applying this approach, the challenge is that you will not ex ante know where this maximum lies.

Assuming that you have worked with budgets for online marketing channels, you can indeed determine your current COS by using the formula above. However, at this point you do not know whether you could achieve more bookings by spending more, while still maintaining the same COS level, or, going the other direction, reduce COS while maintaining the same amount of revenue. That is, you do not know where on the cost-revenue curve your COS actually lies.

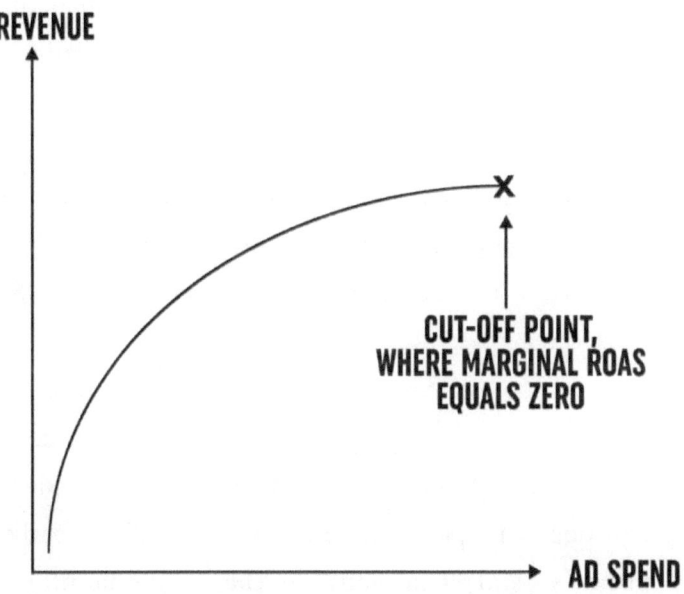

Figure 3 - The Law of Decreasing Marginal Returns on Ad Spend

Hence, to translate the above model into a management tool, I suggest to first defining a maximum COS that you are ready to pay for your direct bookings, above which additional website revenue becomes prohibitively expensive. A good reference point to determine this COS[21] is the average OTA commission for your hotel. Also, you may want to take into account that website bookings encounter divergence losses, such as cancellations (ad spend is lost on these bookings). This can be taken into account in the calculation; however, it is not a necessity.

---

[21] The reservation price of buying website revenue.

If you apply the calculation to stayed revenue, that is revenue that has been actually realized, cancellations are automatically taken into account. Calculating on the basis of booked revenue, that is revenue which has not been realized, is also feasible. However, if you are confronted with high cancellation rates, these should then definitely be part of the equation for calculating the COS for booked revenue.

This is the starting point to determine where you optimum COS lies. Using a trial-and-error approach to ad spend, the optimum COS can now be determined: By adjusting ad spend in the various online marketing channels and constantly tracking, monitoring and analyzing their ROAS, you can now determine what point along the curve is the optimum. Over time, you thus tweak each online marketing channel in order to create the most efficient channel mix. Return this cycle over and over again until you reach a plateau where every additional unit ad spend distorts the actual COS to a level above your maximum COS. Figures 4, 5 and 6 show an example using the above curve, where 10% represented the maximum COS above which additional bookings are considered prohibitively expensive. However, after some tweaking of channels and looking at individual ROAS of each channel it turns out that 8% is actually the optimum COS that can be achieved, where marginal return from additional ad spend is zero. This means that the maximum COS is adjusted to 8% - it does not make sense to increase ad spend in any online marketing channel, because revenue increase is zero. Constantly monitoring this value and testing whether it remains the optimum will then make sure that direct potential is always exhausted.

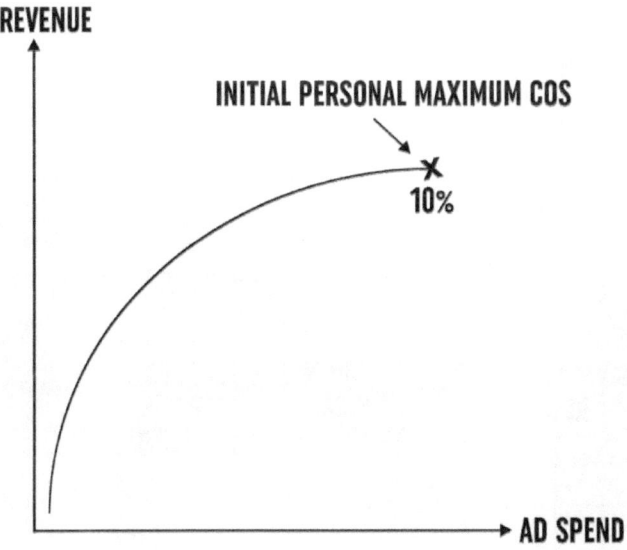

Figure 4 - Initial Maximum COS

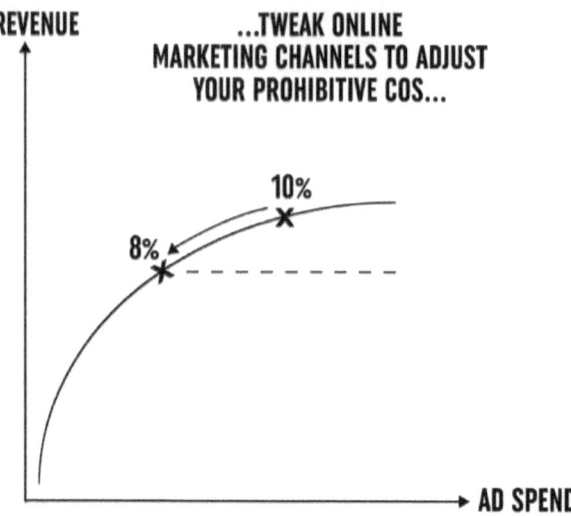

Figure 5 - Adjusted Maximum COS

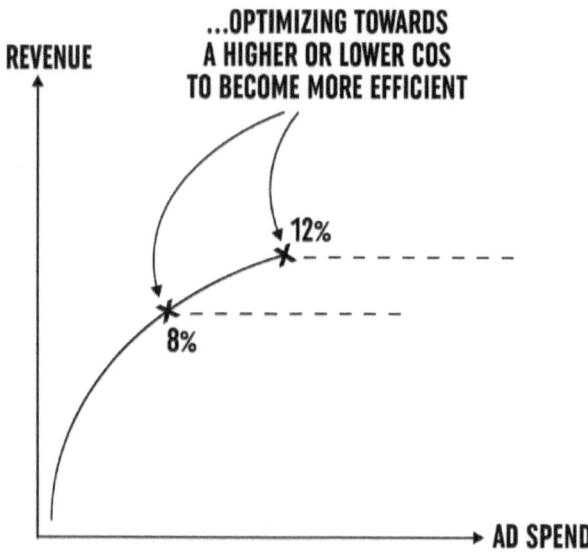

Figure 6 - New Efficient Optimum COS

The trick in this approach is also to understand that website revenue acquired through online marketing directly feeds back into "budget", thus there is no need to worry about a budget in the strict sense, as long as revenue comes in at the optimum COS.

The following six-step guide sums up how to implement the above approach:

1. Determine the actual current COS for direct bookings by summarizing all online marketing spend and calculating the cost-per-order-ratio over revenue.
2. Set a threshold COS (maximum COS) acceptable for direct bookings. Ideally, this is value is at par or just a little below the average OTA commission.
3. Invest into the online marketing channels that seem most promising, whether it be Meta, SEM, SEO, Affiliate or Email up to the amount where the sum of all reaches the maximum COS.
4. Determine the point to which each marketing channel contributes to revenue without pushing the overall COS over the maximum point. If you find that you spend additional money on a channel without increase in revenue, stop or even decrease your spend.

5. After having done 4., recalculate the actual COS – this is the optimum COS.
6. Repeat over again to account for seasonality, competitor behavior and rate/price fluctuations. Constantly manage for better performance in all marketing channels to see whether you can determine a new optimum COS.

With this approach the hotel website as a singular distribution channel is comparable to OTAs, as the costs of a direct booking can be determine with accuracy. In this approach, the limit to the amount of website revenue that can be created is set only be the maximum COS you are willing to pay, freed from the constraints of a marketing budget.

4.3. Cost Differentials and Channel Dependencies in Online Marketing

It also follows from the above that managing for an overall average COS across all online marketing channels, instead of one COS for each channel individually, brings with it superior advantages in the allocation of funds:

Ad spend can be flexibly allocated to the channels with best performance. Instead of scaling down a singular channel because of it severing its individually determined COS-level, and not using the funds saved in other marketing channels, these funds can be re-distributed to where they generate adequate returns. Also, it allows to account for a long-term strategic investment premium in the direct distribution strategy: Allowing the actual COS of a particular marketing channel to remain above the original threshold in order to bring traffic to the website that translates into customer data, such as email-addresses, that can be used to later sell via a less costly channel. For example, creating visibility on metasearch engines can become quite costly, however, they provide good generic traffic - that is users which are not familiar with your hotel / brand yet. Although they might not convert directly, they can be targeted at a later stage via retargeting and email, or they may even come back to the website by entering the domain name directly into the browser address bar. These are all comparatively cheap channels, where conversions will reduce the average COS-value of your website.

COS-values can be calculated for direct website revenue as well as for online marketing channels individually. The costliness of a marketing channel is expressed by the comparison of its average COS (or ROAS) with that of other marketing channels. For example, marketing funds spend on metasearch might generate a ROAS of 5 (or COS of 20%) while search engine marketing produces a ROAS of 10 (or a COS of 10%). When designing an online marketing strategy, including the determination of the optimum COS-value for website revenue as a whole, such cost differentials across channels have to be taken into account, in order to exhaust full revenue potential. An example of cost levels for online marketing channels and how they relate to the overall website COS can be found in Figure 7.

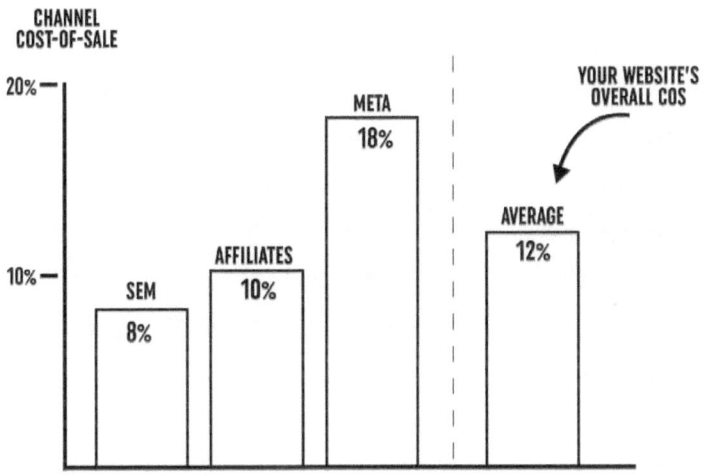

Figure 7 - Cost Differentials of Online Marketing Channels

To achieve an optimum overall COS-value while simultaneously maximizing website revenue, it must be the principle aim of an online marketing strategy to grow direct business first and foremost along the lines of the least costly channels. It stands to reason that this approach makes sense, as the more bookings are produced via less cost intensive channels, the higher the contribution margin of each booking, and the better net operating result will look.

However, there is a second, less obvious fact to this, which relates to the fact of publisher dependency. Direct distribution represents the attempt to grow independent of third party intermediaries, such as OTAs. Thus, you do not want to substitute one dependency through another, that is, become dependent on a specific publisher or search engine for your website traffic. The general rule is that the fewer transactional links between you and your guest a channel includes, the less costly that channel is. This goes hand in hand with a reduced dependency risk. Specifically, the risk of price changes in a channel, i.e. an increase of the CPCs or CPMs demanded by the respective publisher. Such price increases obviously lead to an overall increase of the COS-value in that channel. Hence, the less traffic acquired via a channel in relation to the overall traffic value, the less influence on the overall COS a price increase of that channel will have.

As do most online business models, intermediaries for direct bookings, such as metasearch engines, search engines or social media, have a tendency to build monopolistic structures. For example, consider the worldwide market for search engines: There is Google with a quasi-monopolist position, and Bing comes in second with a fraction of the market share.[22] A similar composition is found in the market for metasearch, where the distribution of market share is highly asymmetric. Usually, more than 60-70% of a hotel's metasearch revenue can be attributed to one metasearch, and

---

[22] See https://www.statista.com/statistics/216573/worldwide-market-share-of-search-engines/

numbers 2 and 3 will most likely not account for more than 10% each. This situation implies, ceteris paribus, an increase in metasearch revenue will increase the dependency on one or two metasearch engines. Although in principle it is a good thing to shift revenue from OTAs to the hotel website by using metasearch because it reduces costs short-term, exposure to distribution dependency risk may not be mitigated: The rise of CPCs. To understand why this is a very relevant risk - which I believe is already manifesting itself in direct distribution - it is necessary to take a closer look at the incentives prevalent in online markets with monopolistic structures. In such markets, the monopolist has the authority to raise prices as he pleases: either because he wants to increase profit or in order maintain to maintain current profitability, in which case he is forced by his own cost structure to raise prices.

For our purpose, the latter reason is the one with relevance to the subject at hand. The connection between dependency on a certain online marketing channel, the cost structure of the respective publishers and the risk of price/COS-increases is illustrated by the concept of "traffic arbitrage". Arbitrage as an economic concept denotes the taking advantage of price differences for the same good in different markets in order to reap profits. In the realms of online marketing, arbitrage, or more accurately traffic arbitrage, takes advantage of differences in prices for clicks. On an abstract level, this is the basic business model of metasearch engines: They acquire traffic and sell it to other websites. For each click on a website that lists on the metasearch, the metasearch receives a payment from that website, i.e. the CPC. This is the sell side of the metasearch business model. However, to be able to sell traffic to websites, metasearches have to acquire traffic in the first place. And here, again, the structure of quasi-monopolistic markets applies: Metasearches are highly dependent on the traffic they acquire via search engines, but also other online marketing channels such as display or affiliate marketing. Hence, their business model is depending on their ability to sell traffic at price higher than the one they pay for that traffic to their "suppliers".[23]

This means that the risk of increasing CPC-cost for any marketing channel has to be accounted for in the channel mix and online marketing strategy. Forward looking, and under the assumption that quasi monopolistic structures in search engine markets remain, this risk seems very high. Considering that paid-for-advertising on search engines will displace organic search results with regard to prominence on search results pages, the competition for

---

[23] This is the reason why metasearches, similar to OTAs, like TV advertising so much: It provides an additional traffic source and reduces the dependency on search engines.

search engine advertising will increase and CPCs will rise. Combined with a general tendency of monopolists to skim monopolist rents – in this context meaning to set base CPCs completely at own discretion – the probability that costs for search engine marketing will rise in the future is high. Hence, the probability that metasearch CPCs will increase is correspondingly high, too.

To mitigate such risks of channel dependency and COS-increase, it is advisable to allocate time and money with a focus on channels that have a low COS. The resulting order of priority in online marketing:

1. SEO hygiene is crucial. The largest share of website traffic still comes from those organic search results and it is absolutely paramount to be among the top positions for brand keywords (such as your hotel name). In addition, improving the website ranking for generic keywords by providing relevant content relating to location, events and certain key services of the hotel, is essential if your website is also to claim top positions for generic keywords.
2. Direct access to the customer is most preferable, that is why extending access to guests via email should be high up on your priority list.
3. Focus on less cost intensive performance marketing measures with high impact on revenue

growth potential. Of these, brand SEM is first, metasearch second and non-brand SEM third.

4. You may enrich your marketing mix with measures that are moderately cost intensive, but limited in revenue impact, such as affiliate marketing and retargeting.
5. If your prohibitive COS is high enough, you may also want to invest in measures that have little direct revenue impact but can create awareness for your brand somewhere along the customer purchase funnel such as display marketing (including programmatic advertising).

The return differential in generic online marketing
Cost differentials in online marketing channels also derive from the competition for clicks in channels, and the return these clicks generate to those competing for them. Naturally, as cost differentials between channels exist, so do differences in ROAS. More "generic" forms of online marketing - that is, forms that cater to the very top end of the customer journey or purchase funnel, with limited targeting and no brand name involved - stand out in a particularly unprofitable way here. The remainder of this chapter is devoted to explaining the particular traits of such broad scale online marketing, and why for most hotels, competing with OTAs on this field - as opposed

to all other forms of online marketing - is highly inefficient.

When compared on the size of their offerings, even the biggest hotel chains are dwarfed by OTAs. On any given destination, an OTA can offer many more hotels, and consequently, more price points than any single hotel or group can. Thus, competing for clicks on high CPC bids is a war that cannot be won. The enormous asymmetry in supply on any given destination between OTA and hotel(s) implies that with mathematical certainty, the differences in conversion potential for traffic from generic SEM is significantly higher for OTAs. From this follows that the return on ad spend - ceteris paribus - is higher for OTAs. Consider a simple example: How many hotels can the largest hotel chain offer in a destination, such as, e.g. Paris or New York? How many hotels can an OTA offer in that same destination? The size of the OTA offering exceeds even the largest hotel groups, which explains why OTAs able to leverage returns from ad spend on generic search terms, such as "Hotel New York". The condensed availability of offers in one central place reduces search and transaction costs for users tremendously. If price cancels out as the purchase decision driver because it is the same across all distribution channels, this reduction in search costs allows OTAs to convert visitors to bookers on any given destination at a higher rate. In technical terms, OTAs can create much larger economies of scale in selling online, as compared to hotels.

This is why OTAs are also able to effectively use marketing measures with high waste effects, such as TV, programmatic advertising, and generic SEM. Their huge portfolio is able to absorb a large portion of the audience they reach. This absorb/spend ratio is far beyond what any hotel can reach. Only the biggest worldwide hotel chains can reach ratios where investing in marketing such as TV becomes a viable investment and even they are far less effective in reaching target audiences.

Understanding this basic relationship in online marketing for hotels is the key to an efficient direct distribution strategy. There are some means of "generic" online marketing where money will simply burn away with little to no effect on revenue. An intermixture of these means in your online marketing mix makes sense only when all other means are effectively exhausted, and the expectation for return from such campaigns is lowered accordingly.

4.4. Without Rate Parity, Everything is Nothing

Regardless of what marketing instruments you choose, where you allocate your ad spend and how sophisticated your ads are, it all vanishes in the face of irresponsible pricing and distribution. Even the most advanced websites and marketing instruments will not be powerless and not bring in more direct bookings, if rooms are sold on other channels at discounted rates that are do not available on the hotel website. What looks like a no-brainer is, however, not a matter of course in the hotel industry. Reason being that historically, this industry never had a concept for direct distribution until e-commerce stepped on the scene in beginning of the 2000's. The hotel industry as always relied on a multitude of sales channels, often without explicitly understanding how these sales channels actually work. When OTAs entered the distribution market, the industry to a large extend missed out on analyzing how the business model of an OTA actually functions, but simply looked at the amount of rooms filled, not going beyond and looking at *how* these rooms are filled.

This is why it is necessary to lay out the economics of online distribution, as a basis for understanding why *rate parity of a hotel website is the most important factor in online distribution*. As a heuristic, consider the following three characteristics as the most determining economic features of online distribution:

Perfect Market conditions apply. Markets are considered perfect when information on prices is available at any time to all market participants in full transparency. Understand that in the online world - with search engines, metasearches and highly designed websites - everything is transparent and comparable at a mouse click. This means that the consumer has perfect information available at any point in time. Thus, if you are doing an OTA promotion or flash sale, you must know about the mechanisms in online marketing. Be aware of the fact that online, everything is in competition at every second. Online marketing must be concerted around these circumstances, bids have to be adjusted mailings setup and campaigns turned on or off, depending on demand and competition. Managing online marketing effectively requires full attention to your entire distribution landscape and an understanding of how the different distribution channels - such as OTAs, flash seller, tour operator, wholesale, etc. - act, where they are strong and where they can exploited.

Visibility is the currency of the online world, and everyone chases it. All online marketing activities have one principle in common: they try to make a product or service *visible*. Visibility in this sense is a market, too. On the supply side, there are those who offer visibility – social media, metasearch, search engines and the like. The power to "make visible" is usually concentrated in very few hands. On the demand side, however, the actors are numerous. OTAs and hotel websites are eager to offer cash in return for visibility. This is why Google, Facebook and Co. are piling mountains of cash by the second - their seller bargaining power is extremely high. Hence, the more actors compete for visibility, the higher the prices the supply side can command in return. OTAs have understood this early and are willing to throw horrendous amounts of money after these supply side enablers, just to stay visible.

Supply chains are complex and branch out endlessly

Between the final selling point of a rate, such as an OTA, and the hotel that actually distributes the rate, the number of involved parties can easily surpass four, five and even more. The reason for this is found in most hotels' very own distribution structure. For the most part, hotels still work with complex rate structures, distributing rates at different prices according to the type of distributor they are *directly* working with. Alas, different prices for tour operators, bed banks, OTAs, GDS and direct distribution. Adding to complexity are regional, tax and booking-terms-based differences in pricing. Online, such diverse rate structure does often not follow the path a hotel may have foreseen (if it gave consideration to the distribution value chain at all). Consider the following example: A hotel gives a certain rate to a bed bank. It is a net rate and allows the bed bank to add its own, discretionary mark-up to it. The bed bank then passes the rate on to some OTA, which in turn feeds it into its affiliate program where some small-weird-name OTA grabs it and places it on a metasearch website. At exactly this point, the hotel's own website will have to compete with the rate, because it is being compared on the metasearch.

However, control over distribution is lost the moment the rate is passed to the bed bank without restrictions. Hence, the different players along the distribution chain may play with their margin, reducing it to a few percent, thus heavily undercutting the hotel website price. Of course, a sound way to overcome such cases of arbitrage business is to cut off at the root of the problem. The most reliable way is to simply stop cooperating/contracting with the respective 1st level distributor (in the example above, the bed bank). However, most hoteliers are lacking the guts to do so. The argument posted against such a distribution weed out is often: "But distribution channel such and such is responsible for x amount of revenue and I cannot cut him off." Well that may be true, but how do you think this distributor generates this amount of revenue? The point is that these distributors are only able to generate revenue because they sell online - and take a healthy bite from the revenue cake that is supposed to be your websites'. To illustrate this relationship between supply and demand online, Figure 8 draws on the analogy of a bloated gut - while visibility vis a vis the consumer/user is controlled by few (B, search engines, metasearch, social media) and rate distribution is initiated by one (A, the hotel), the distribution chain in between is overloaded with a variety of actors that want to get a piece of the action. This is the bloated gut - it is completely unnecessary in getting rates from A to B because with its own website, the hotel can go directly to B without incurring further costs of distribution.

Hence, cutting off or reducing such distribution partners off in the long run represents an important lever for growing direct distribution revenue. Online economics are on your side in this case: Simply calculating the value of third party commissions saved and opportunity costs off handing out cheap net rates shows that even with slight revenue dips incurred from closing certain distribution channels, the compensation from direct website bookings will more than compensate potential losses on the contribution margin.

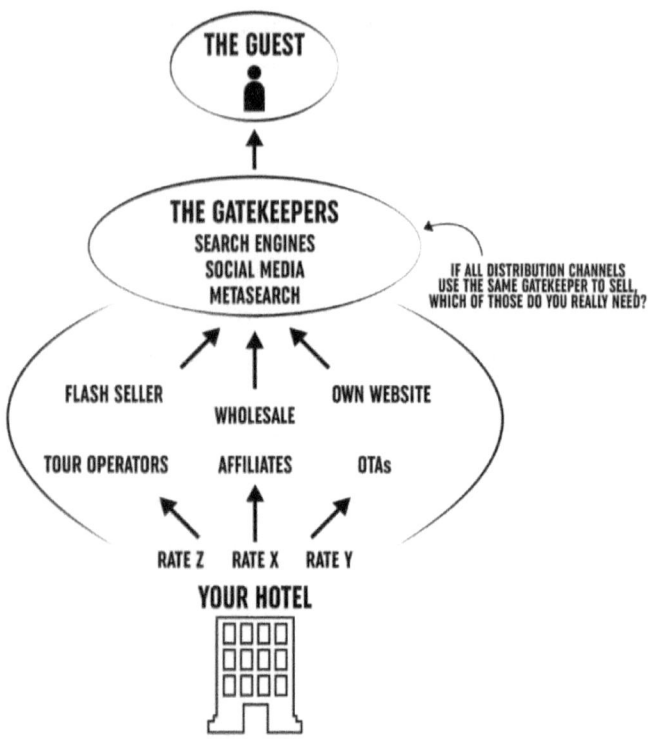

Figure 8 - The Bloated Gut Problem in Online Distribution

In combination, the three factors create an extremely competitive environment, where mistakes in pricing and distribution are punished immediately. So when you come across websites undercutting your own website's rate by 30%, remember that it all starts in your hotel. It is in your hands to correct such differences and align all rates on the market to one level. No user will book on your website if he can find your rooms at a cheaper price elsewhere. Once rates are passed on to distribution partners, they will show up online at some point and they will be in direct competition with the rates of direct distribution. Reclaiming authority over distribution is essential to direct booking success, and the key to doing so is *rate parity* - that is, the rates found on a hotel website always have to meet the lowest rate on the market. Better yet, these rates are the best on the market at any point in time.

Sensible pricing is complemented by a rigorous approach to room availability on the own website. One of the most important lessons for online marketing for hotels is still: *Never close the availability of your website* (unless occupancy is at 100% and more, of course. Guests should learn over time that there is always a room left on the hotel website, even when all other channels have no availability left. Aside from positively impacting the COS, as over time, guests/users will start include a hotel website among the first touch points of the customer journey, as they learn to find best prices and last room availability there. This reflects in a decreasing effective COS, as ad spend used for acquisition of traffic becomes more efficient over time. Hence, unless you are overbooked and your website should always be open, everything else should be closed before.[24]

---

[24] This is also why a hotel should desist from giving allotments to distribution partners. While the website may be closed already, there may be other rooms left / blocked for distribution partners. Typically, these rooms can be sold at a higher price than the

---

allotment prices - which are usually fixed price - leaving the hotel at a loss on the revenue (rooms get sold for lower rates than the market price) as well as the cost side (direct distribution is still the least costly form of distribution).

4.5. Timing of Marketing Measures

One of the most important tasks of an online marketer is to know when to make use of a given marketing channel, that is, finding the right moment for a campaign. The main objective in timing is to find the best channel for maximum performance by allocating funds the those channels with the highest return, or lowest cost-per-order value. Timing is relevant, because some marketing channels work better than others in certain situations with regards to their cost-benefit-ratio. For example, one marketing channel may be superior to another with regard to conversion rate and hence overall revenue, or it may surpass another by its cost-per-order value. Hence, deciding for the right channel - or a combination of channels - at the right time leads to improved revenue results and cost/revenue-ratios.

Timing online marketing for hotels, there are two simple rules to follow, which will lead you to an optimum of direct booking revenue and direct distribution cost.

The first one rather simple: Pull Marketing (search engine marketing, metasearch and retargeting) should be "always on". Pulling demand that is already out there is easier than generating demand in the first place. You do not want to miss the chance of pulling in a user that has displayed interest. This is why constant visibility on search engines, and to a lesser extend metasearch, is of paramount importance. Retargeting also falls into this category, because it addresses those users that have already been in contact with your website.

The second rule is more complex and requires the introduction another concept, whose use in the hospitality industry is most astonishing to me. The disputable concept in question is what I call "Anyway Business". Anyway Business is business that I have without taking any active effort of bringing in the business. A good example for this concept is the online marketer asking the hotel manager (or the person responsible for filling rooms): "What kind of price campaign can we do next month?" The manager responds: "Well, I do not need a price campaign, because I have so much business (or occupancy, for that matter) *anyway*." The problem with this concept is that it completely ignores the perspective of cost-of-acquisition: Filling your rooms with costly OTA or tour operator business might not be the best option when you are looking at optimizing bottom line. Anyway Business is easy, because it does not require any active action, you simply plug in a third party and your rooms get sold. In the perspective of Anyway Business costs are generously overlooked, since only revenue and occupancy are considered. This will to lead to suboptimal results on the bottom line.

Rather, I suggest using a cost-per-order approach to filling rooms, starting with the least costly acquisition channel. Overall, this requires you to know the cost of acquisition for all of your online and offline channels. However, as an example, looking exclusively at website bookings shall suffice and will illustrate the idea of the concept. The underlying idea is that for every online marketing channel, there exists a profit-optimal price at its given marginal cost level. Accordingly, less costly channels have relatively more leeway in pricing than more costly channels. It follows that the least costly channels should have the best rates, in order for these channels to fill rooms first. In this logic, the other, more expensive channels subsequently stack up on occupancy, until the desired combination of occupancy-level & revenue is reached. An example of this approach is shown in Figure 9. Three marketing channels are considered: email, SEM and metasearch. Given the varying cost differentials between these channels, margins (revenue minus ad spend) will also vary. With increasing occupancy, the leeway to increase prices increase and more expensive channels can be used to fill rooms. Vice versa, the most attractive rates should be distributed in the least costly channels first, where margins are highest after subtracting ad spend/cost from rate/price.

In using this approach, the idea of anyway business becomes obsolete in timing of marketing campaigns. Timing campaigns thus moves away from trying to fill rooms in times of need (that is, times when there is no "Anyway Business") to managing campaigns solely on their probability to provide a high contribution margin. Manage for profit, not occupancy and revenue. If online marketing channels are managed accordingly, you will come to acknowledge the benefits of bookings from email campaigns and SEO very fast.

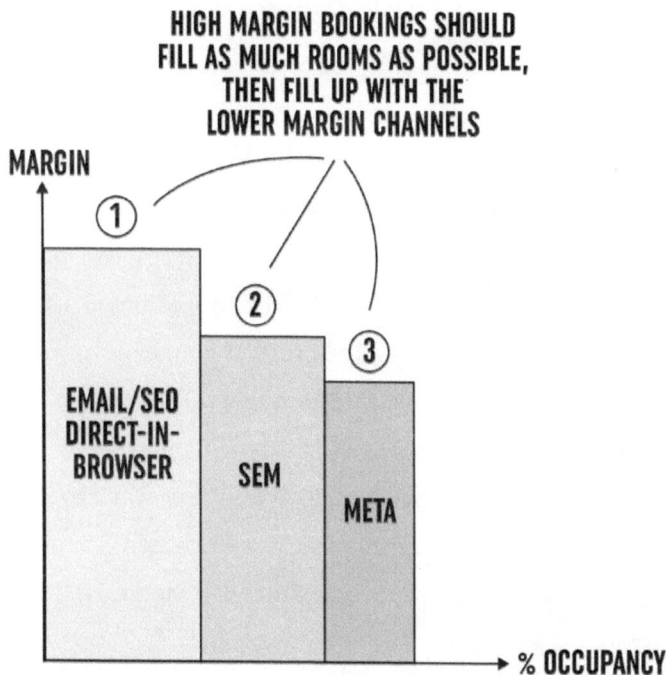

Figure 9 - Best Price for High Margin Channels

Making a Case for Increased Spending on Online Marketing in High Demand Periods

Fellows sceptic of direct bookings, who are not willing to invest in online marketing for a hotel website, often try to kill increased ad spend with the following argument: "Selling in high demand periods is easy, anybody can do it. It is the need periods we need to focus on! And this is where your website cannot deliver. Business outside of need periods I do get anyway, so why should I spend more on online marketing of create exclusive rates for my website?" Although it may seem reasonable at first, there is a strong fallacy underlying this statement. In order to detect it, one must take the overarching perspective that only a thought-through distribution strategy can provide. Since you have already bought this book and made it to this chapter, I am assuming here that you want to increase your share in direct website bookings. Why do you want to do so? You want to reduce the financial burden that OTA commissions place on you and you want to reduce your dependency on third party distribution in the long run. If this is your goal, ask yourself whether the above statement is still persuasive and sensible. You may already realize that it is not. To identify its flaw one must simply understand the laws of supply and demand and visibility on the internet. When demand is high and prices go up, hotels are able to command higher rates. This means that the return on marketing invest for any given booking in this period goes up, as there is more money to be made by advertisers. Thus, prices for marketing space (i.e. visibility) go up, as advertisers are more willing to spend in order to "get that booking" – CPCs, CPOs, CPMs etc. go up. Now, because of the high average value of these bookings you want to get exactly those, because this is where the money is. Do not waste too much time and money selling what is left on the rummage table. Now, the argument goes that "I get this (money) business in any event, I do not need a hotel website (and online marketing) for that" – yes, you do get it, but at what price? Would you rather spend 18% on a 1000 Dollar booking on OTA commission or 15% in online marketing for your own website? The more business you are able to drive to your own website, the less dependent you become on OTAs and the more self-sustaining your distribution will be. This is exactly why you should focus on attracting the high value business to your own website. Doing so requires a willingness to invest in marketing in high demand periods - rest assured that OTAs will do so. In order to compete with them for the high value business on metasearches and search engines, you have to be able to adjust your bids for clicks, and consequently short-term spending in online marketing. You should avoid thinking in budgets but if you must, you should prioritize for high demand seasons. You rather want to be out of budget in "need periods" than in high demand periods. Leave the need periods to flash dealers, they are happy to pick them up for you.

4.6. Online Marketing for Mobile

Contemporary studies highlight the growing relevance of mobile device use and consequently, mobile marketing. Mobile marketing receives a significant push from published studies by large publishers and the like[25], showing that use of mobile devices to access websites has double digit growth rates every year and will exceed the one of desktops in the near future. Basically, for mobile marketing the same truths hold as for desktop marketing, however, with a few peculiarities that make it worth being examined in a separate chapter. In principal, there is no difference between desktop and mobile with regard to the management of e.g. metasearch, SEO, and SEM and the like. However, mobile marketing still has a dedicated position in the customer journey, very often at the beginning of the customer journey. Truth is that although the use of mobile devices for engaging in online research and inspiration for travel increases, the tendency to book mobile does not. Hence, as the number of touch points increases, the *potential* exposure to marketing increases, too. This bears the risk is that advertisers end

---

[25] See, for example, http://think.storage.googleapis.com/docs/micromoments-guide-to-winning-shift-to-mobile-download.pdf and http://www.criteo.com/de/wp-content/uploads/sites/3/2018/03/Criteo-Q4-Travel-Insights-DE.pdf required

up paying multiple times for the acquisition of one booker, thereby increasing the COS, sometimes significantly.

Since conversion rates on mobile devices are low, the acquisition of mobile bookings is principally more expensive than for desktop bookings. Now, suppose you engage in mobile marketing and you might acquire a user via search engine marketing, which creates a certain CPC-cost. Suppose you cannot convert the user directly, as he is early in his customer journey and does not intend to book directly on his mobile device. One or two days later, he returns to his journey via a desktop device, and again clicks on your advertisement creating costs. Suppose the user eventually books, you end up paying twice for the acquisition of his booking.

Now, one might hold against this the fact that even in cases where a customer engages only in desktop activity, he too might click twice on a search engine ad before booking and create acquisition costs. This argument was to be valid if it reflected the reality of desktop use for booking hotels online. However, the typical booking process does reflect this idea: Once a user has accessed a website via a marketing ad, returning visits tend to be via direct type in of the website domain, by using a bookmark, or clicking in a relatively low priced retargeting ad. Between mobile and desktop, this re-access is difficult to achieve (although not impossible). Hence, the probability for paying multiple times for the same user is higher in customer journeys that include multiple devices and, ceteris paribus, the COS is higher in a multiple-device journey than in a desktop-only journey.

It follows that the place for mobile marketing in your overall online heavily depends on your ability to convert mobile traffic directly. Odds are that your conversion rate on mobile devices - even with a super-performing mobile optimized website - will be comparatively low (less than 0.8%) or even very low (less than 0.5%). With such ratios, the economic use of mobile marketing becomes a question of your prohibitive COS-value. For instance, a maximum COS between 12 and 15% will not allow generating significant revenue volume with a mobile conversion rate of 0.5%, *unless* room rates are extremely high.

The central question in mobile advertising is whether it becomes possible to increase the conversion rate of mobile devices for hotel bookings. It might be the case that it is simply a question of users getting used to booking mobile, and hence conversion rates on mobile devices are subsequently improving over time. Thus, unless you are able to actively push mobile conversion rates above 1.0%, dedicated mobile marketing measures can receive a subordinate position in your overall online marketing. Thus, mobile marketing should be considered an integral part of all online marketing channels, however, it is not necessary to create a separate mobile strategy for online marketing.

4.7. Vouchers & Promotional Codes

Vouchers and promotional codes are a powerful weapon in the fight for direct website bookings. Their principal mechanism is to reduce price, as do promotional codes, or to add an allowance to a booking, such as e.g. F&B vouchers. Obviously, both tools can additional leverage to your online marketing campaigns. To fully understand how and when to make use of them in campaigns, however, requires a deeper look at their functionality:

1. Vouchers provide instant gratification: Saving money - or the promise of saving money - is a direct incentive to purchase a good or service. This is particularly relevant for the younger generation of customers, whose tolerance for time delay in receiving gratification is extremely low. Instant gratification for the booker through direct cash value gives you a competitive edge over "pure" offerings.

2. Vouchers are distributed with exclusivity. By attaching the reception to a desired action, one can steer booking behavior. A good use-case here is to build up your email-distribution list. E.g., by rewarding website visitors with a voucher for

leaving their email address with you, a desired action is triggered.

3. Both can be used in special campaigns and short-term sales activities, without having to interfere with the overall rate structure / revenue management for all channels. Hence, vouchers allow online marketing to act independently of revenue management.

4. Positive nominal values in a currency (e.g. EUR or USD) are much easier to grasp by most people than percentages. E.g., giving someone a 100 EUR voucher on a booking of 1,000 EUR works better than a 10%-price cut on the same 1,000 EUR booking, although technically the result for the booker is the exact same. Whereas price changes in rates must usually be expressed in %-off values – for either management or technical reasons – vouchers can also make use of nominal values.

There are basically three types of vouchers, but experience shows that they are not all equally effective. Ranked for effectiveness in pushing sales, the three types are:

1. *Cash value vouchers* (e.g. " Get a 100 EUR F&B voucher with your next booking")
2. *%-off vouchers* (e.g. "Save 10% on your next booking by entering the code XYZ")
3. *Vouchers for Products/Services* (e.g. "Get a free massage with your next stay")

They may not be the sexiest form of marketing, but vouchers definitely work and provide you with a great tool for driving short term direct revenue.

4.8. A Hotel Website is a Shop, not a Digital Brochure

Although this is not a book on website and booking engine design, I feel it is necessary to refer to some basic principles for hotel websites in order to prevent readers from wasting their online marketing efforts. Because naturally, if your website is dysfunctional, all the hard acquired traffic will bounce off.

One of the most misunderstood things about hotel in the hotel industry is function they fulfill: Still, too many hoteliers confuse a website for a digital brochure of their hotel. That is, they believe a good website is characterized by its appeal to "emotion", "brand image", or even their personal whims about style and design. The problem with this approach to website design is that it does not acknowledge the fundamental difference between *selling* and *imaging*. If you look at the most successful websites in e-commerce, such as amazon or booking.com, they are hardly masterpieces of aesthetics. However, they are economically successful because the companies that operate them understand their purpose: *to sell*. These websites work because they cater to the need of their users in any particular moment: to find a product, to book a service or to send a request. These tasks demand effort on the side of the user, and the less effort is necessary to complete them, the more likely it is that the user finds his need fulfilled and actually converts from browsing to booking.

Understanding this is elementary to any successful hotel website design. Too many hoteliers still share the misconception that a website should be "fun" or "entertaining" or be "emotional" (without ever defining what this actually means). Of course, this is a principally legitimate way to view the purpose of a website. However, it is not logically consistent with wanting more direct revenue. Believe it or not, for most people, booking a hotel is not a joyous thing to do. It is a necessity through which most users want to get as quickly as possible, without spending much energy on it. The actual task of booking the hotel is a phase of exhaustion: Comparing prices, pictures, location and amenities requires attention on the part of the user. Attention requires energy and the less energy is required to book a hotel, the more likely it is that the hotel actually gets booked. Booking a room on your website must be done so effortless that the user does not even realize he is booking a room until he reaches the "book now"- button. Internalize that a website is either a shop or a picture book, but there is no in between.

Thus my advice is to follow a number of proven e-commerce principles that have demonstrated bring about high conversion rates:

> **Always: Less is more!** Perfection is when there is nothing redundant left. Try to keep content and function on any page in line with the purpose of the page - what is the user actually looking for on the particular page? If he is looking to book a room, there is no need to overload him with pictures, funky visual effects or loads of happy talk texts.

> **Keep relevant information easily accessible.** Do not use overly fancy navigations, call-to-actions, slide galleries etc. These will eventually annoy the user, because they demand more interaction from him. Interaction (i.e. looking and clicking) demands effort and is exhausting. The more effort it takes to navigate through a website, the less likely it will be that users will book on it.

> **One call-to-action at a time.** Each page should present at the maximum one or two call-to-actions. More will be confusing and also lead to the user finally leaving your website exhausted and annoyed.

> **Do not hide the booking widget!** The booking widget (where users enter stay information such

as dates and number of guests) is the most important part of a hotel website. On pages where users actually intend to look at prices or book directly, the booking widget is the key entry point to the booking engine and should have the most prominent spot on the page.

> **Keep your booking engine lean.** The booking engine (IBE) is the heart of your website. If you can afford to build your own, try to keep it intuitive and try to use as few clicks as possible from entry point to "book now". If you take an off-the-shelf IBE, you will probably not have the opportunity to bring in your own ideas on its design, so you should check beforehand, if its design sticks to the principles above.

4.9. A Brief Excursion Into A/B-Testing

Testing elements of a website or media asset in order to optimize towards click- and conversion-rates is common practice in e-commerce, most generally referred to as A/B-Testing. In A/B Testing, variations of elements, such as pictures, taglines and descriptions, are tested against each other in order to find out whether one variation (A) has a better performance than another (B) in regard to a predefined indicator, such as the click-through rate or the conversion rate. There are two areas of interest, where testing can be applied:

1. Website
2. Advertisements

A/B testing a website or advertisement includes testing variations of any element that in one way or another impacts the user behavior: colors, shapes, positions to entirely different variations of webpages. For our purpose, the first is of particular relevance and will receive be put under scrutiny.

Although not strictly part of online marketing, A/B-testing a website is related to it in that it tries to improve the revenue extracted from traffic acquired via online marketing. As there is a lot of buzz revolving around the idea of A/B testing, and a lot of software services for A/B testing are sold to hoteliers, it is addressed here also. Software that promises to increase revenue by making better use of website visitors is abundant in the hospitality industry. Such tools try to convert more visitors into bookers, by testing all elements of a website, such as colors, design, structure, headlines etc., then analyzing the resulting data on clicks and conversions, and ultimately determining the best performing elements or combinations thereof. This should bring about a fully conversion optimized website over time, as continuous testing leads to finding the optimum for each element on a website. To preclude, I consider that that for most hotel websites conversion optimization is a waste of time and money. Generally, price and room availability are much more powerful factors in driving up conversion rates than are button positions, colors or call-to-action wording. Although these sure have relevance, they tend to be highly overhyped by A/B-testing. The companies offering such software market their relevance accordingly, promising a holy grail of conversion rate increase. Granted, the story around conversion rate optimization is very seductive. Enhanced with sophisticated mathematics, A/B Testing promises more sales and more revenue beyond the application of simple truths like keeping a hotel website's price the best in the market. What is often concealed, however, is the fact that for single hotels, or hotel chains with just a few hotels selling on one website, A/B-testing has often very limited to no value because of a statistical law: Traffic volumes on a hotel website are simply too small to achieve statistically valid results from A/B-testing over acceptable periods of time. Unless monthly visitors are in the hundreds of thousands, it will simply take too long to reach valid results. You end up running A/B-Tests for months before achieving statistical relevance of the results. It is important to understand where website testing originated: It was first applied by the leading e-commerce websites - such as the major OTAs - which are able to raise up massive amounts of website traffic for testing purposes. With visitors in the hundreds of thousands or millions, it is comparatively easy to achieve statistical relevance in A/B- tests.

Most hotel websites, however, are distinctively different from general e-commerce or OTA websites in that they do not enjoy the traffic volumes of statistically relevant dimensions necessary to get valid results from testing. In any type of A/B-Testing, large volumes of observations are necessary to achieve statistically valid results. Reason being that in large volumes, the impact of a single observation is very limited and outliers cannot distort the result. When just few observations exist, the impact of a single observation is high and it can distort the average into a completely wrong interpretation.

For example, compare two cases with differing number of observations, for example, in a test of two different button colors to increase conversion rate. In the first case, the test counts 100 observations and one conversion, hence $1/100 = 0.01$. In the second case, the test counts 4,000 observations and 40 conversions, hence $40/4,000 = 0.01$. In both cases the interpretation of the result could be the same: both color tests show the same conversion rate.

However, what happens to the resulting conversion rate if we add one more observation with a conversion to the result? In the second case, we have $41/4,001 = 0.01025$. The conversion rate is almost not affected by this additional conversion. In the first case however, the result is quite different: $2/101 = 0.0198$, which means that the conversion rate almost doubled because of this single additional observation. A/B-Testing variables on the ground of limited traffic (i.e. observations does not make sense - the risk of coming to a wrong conclusion on what variant of the variable performs better is simply too high. Only with an increase in observations does the result become valid for interpretation. Figure 10 illustrates this context in a simplified way.

My philosophy is thus to stick to very few simple design laws that are tried and trusted when initially setting up a website: Clean design, clear and few call-to-actions, up-to-date and lots of picture material and a small number of room-rate combinations in the booking engine. Once these design principles are implemented on a hotel website, there should be little concern with further A/B-Testing and UX design. As a hotelier with a limited budget, it is sensible to rather invest in performance marketing budget than in testing software. If you want to increase direct bookings and direct revenue, you should use your limited financial means to invest in the acquisition of additional (quality) traffic – i.e. performance marketing – rather than trying to make better use of existing traffic – i.e. conversion optimization.

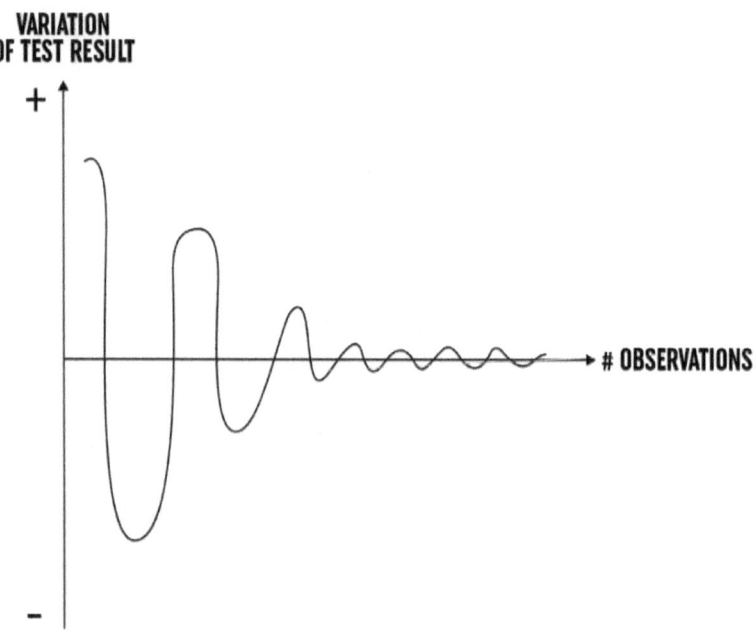

Figure 10 - Variance in A/B Testing

5. Closing Words

By laying out the underlying mechanisms of online marketing for hotels, I tried to provide a framework for formulating growth strategies for direct bookings. For anyone wanting to take direct distribution seriously, this framework provides a proven concept to increase bookings and revenue on hotel websites, thereby reducing the burden of OTA commissions and taking back authority for room distribution. It works for chains and single hotels alike, as the presented fundamentals of online marketing are the same for all hotel types.

Nonetheless, there are of course always specifics to any commercial offering, such as your particular hotel in your particular market. Such specifics cannot be exhaustively covered by any general theory, as by definition a general theory will lose its applicability once it becomes too narrowly focused on details of situations in any point in time. However, what it can do is provide a guide for testing and varying actions such as to make them most effective to the particular situation at hand. In other words, you should always test what online marketing measures work the best for *you* in order to achieve *the particular goal that you* are focusing on, before applying these measures blindly. Testing different marketing measures and combinations requires an understanding of the core mechanisms of online marketing and how they work. My intention in writing this book is to help you develop this understanding.

Getting more direct bookings on your website, decreasing OTA commissions and taking charge of your distribution is not done overnight. It takes time and requires you to think strategically with foresight in the future. Being solely driven by the pressure to achieve next week's budgeted occupancy will drive your view away from any strategic thinking. If you want to achieve *sustainable* growth, occupancy and net result, you have free yourself for a moment from short term thinking. Look at the online marketing measures presented in this book and structure a strategy from it. Ask yourself how you can apply the insights you gathered by reading this book to your specific situation. Ask yourself, what metasearch provider is most relevant to your feeder markets, whether you have the financial resources to bid on generic SEM in limited markets to promote your brand, or in what way you can incentivize guests do sign up for your email distribution list.

Recognize that the mixture of means presented in this book is your direct way to more independence in your distribution, but it requires invest of time and money. In writing this book I also tried to do away with the popular belief among hoteliers that direct bookings come at no charge. Understanding how online markets work implies understanding that direct bookings cost money. Visibility and clicks are the desired goods of the online world and you must invest real money to get them. Hence, you should always calculate the real cost for each direct booking. It is a question of comparative cost whether a direct booking is "better" than an OTA booking. There are two points of view in this cost comparison, both being equally important. One view on this cost comparison is short-term: comparing the direct costs, looking at which one is lower and then making a decision. The other is long-term: what is the price you are willing to pay – i.e. what premium above your OTA commission level are willing to pay – for each direct booking in order to bind guests to your website and have them book directly for future bookings? Are you willing to pay such a premium at all? Presenting your brand directly, providing exclusives offers and acquisition of customer data gives you greater flexibility and opportunities for future revenue generation through cross- & up-selling and making future sales. This opportunity does not exist with OTA bookings, where the OTA controls the customer relationship to a large extend. Obviously, the more you rely on OTA bookings the smaller this opportunity becomes. Furthermore, you should include the price of dependency into this long term few: every OTA booking makes the OTA delivering it stronger in the long term. When deciding on the maximum you are willing to spend per direct booking, it is of utmost importance to also include the latter consideration into the calculation, if you aim at sustainable direct booking growth. Focusing only on the short-term level of cost per direct booking in comparison to OTA commissions may curtail you reaching the full direct potential.

Deriving an online marketing strategy from its framework and implementing it requires time, you may need to hire talent that is able to execute your strategy and you may have to free up budget for some initial investments. But these efforts will be guaranteed to be worthwhile in the long run as they allow adding an elementary building block for the long term safeguarding of the profitability of your business. Neglecting direct bookings, or the distribution via your own website to be more precise, can be fatal. The distribution market for hotels is consolidating, with ever fewer agents increasing their market share, on a global scale. With the internet's tendency to build oligopolistic or quasi-monopolistic markets, hotels that neglect their direct distribution will find them confronted with 1-2 major distributors owning disproportionally large shares of their sales. Such a dependency brings hotels in the uncomfortable situation of having their costs of distribution dictated upon them. Given that the trend of hotel distribution to online channels will not reverse, the risk of ending up in such an adverse power constellation will also increase over time. This book laid out a toolset that helps hotels to actively work against this development. My hope is that the tools presented in this little book help the reader on the way reclaiming distribution authority.

www.ingramcontent.com/pod-product-compliance
Lightning Source LLC
Chambersburg PA
CBHW021408210526
45463CB00001B/270